IGNITING CHILDREN'S WRITING

BLOOMSBURY EDUCATION
Bloomsbury Publishing Plc
50 Bedford Square, London, WC1B 3DP, UK

BLOOMSBURY, BLOOMSBURY EDUCATION and the Diana logo are trademarks of
Bloomsbury Publishing Plc

A catalogue record for this book is available from the British Library

ISBN: PB: 978-1-4729-5158-8; ePDF: 978-1-4729-5159-5; ePub: 978-1-4729-5160-1

2 4 6 8 10 9 7 5 3 1

Text design by Marcus Duck

Printed and bound in the UK by Ashford Colour Press

All papers used by Bloomsbury Publishing Plc are natural, recyclable products from wood grown
in well managed forests. The manufacturing processes conform to the environmental regulations
of the country of origin

To find out more about our authors and books visit www.bloomsbury.com and sign up for
our newsletters

IGNITING CHILDREN'S WRITING

MARK McCAUGHAN

BLOOMSBURY EDUCATION

LONDON OXFORD NEW YORK NEW DELHI SYDNEY

CONTENTS

T: TRY OUT INDIVIDUAL CHOICES

E: EDIT, PERFORM, PUBLISH

RV: REVIEW KEY LEARNING

INTRODUCTION

At best, writing empowers pupils, encouraging them to express themselves and allowing them to proudly present what they've learnt and ideas they've had. For many children, however, writing presents a barrier which stands between them and their potential. When writing is seen by pupils as a barrier, motivating them to do it to the best of their ability is a real challenge for teachers. Sprinkle into the mix a 201-page Key Stage 1 and 2 National Curriculum with its heavy content and lengthy, technical appendices; sweeping changes to assessment; the pressure of end of Key Stage tests in reading and grammar, punctuation and spelling, and the level of challenge for these teachers increases even further.

So, how *do* we manage all the content, the subjects, time, planning, marking and *still* get our pupils to write well? Where we don't succeed, this could be because these pressures have resulted in the different elements of the English curriculum being separated and compartmentalised on the timetable. What a shame to find a secluded spelling scheme slot on Tuesday, a reclusive reading session on a Wednesday and a glum grammar intervention group during assembly on a Friday – all working in perfect isolation when the skills being taught would work together. Other issues could include the curriculum being narrowed; that there is dominance of one-off lessons and worksheets; that the technical aspects of the curriculum have been allowed to dominate; that a planning scheme or product has disengaged the teacher from their own planning; that the majority of writing pieces are 'stand-alone', undrafted and unedited; or that independent writing evidence is compromised by too much teacher input. These disjointed approaches often lead to disjointed writing, which is not informed or inspired by skills and learning from across the curriculum.

What's the answer? This lies in the most dynamic classrooms, where there is joined-up thinking and the skills of writing, reading, spelling, talking and listening are embedded into wonderful teaching sequences, inspired by brilliant texts, which make links between subjects, skills, experiences and the real world. In my experience, these are the classrooms in which the best writing is produced.

Igniting Children's Writing supports teachers to create these sequences, guiding their pupils through the journey from word-level activities to reading tasks, through drafting 'messy' writing by experimenting with writing choices to arriving at an edited and polished piece. This collection is the collation of the ideas I have found work best in supporting pupils to write well. All the activities have been tried and tested in classrooms. They will support pupils to think, talk and read before, whilst and after they write, and to make independent choices as they develop their own distinctive writing voice.

A FERTILE LEARNING ENVIRONMENT

The seeds of even the best teaching ideas can fall on stony ground if the learning environment is not fertile, so it's worth considering the following points:

1 Your top priority should be to establish a reading culture in and beyond your classroom. I wouldn't necessarily recommend anything by Stephen King as a Key Stage 2 text, but he has some good advice about writing: "If you don't have time to read, you don't have the time (or the tools) to write. Simple as that". We, as teachers, should play a major role in helping pupils to read and love great writing because what they read will inspire their writing. In my experience, the best writing is inspired by planning around brilliant texts. And once you've got a brilliant text igniting the learning, you can end each day by reading it with the class, sending the pupils home with a head full of unanswered questions.

A recommended starting point for choosing texts is The CILIP Carnegie and Kate Greenaway Medals (**www. carnegiegreenaway. org.uk**). The first piece of advice I give new subject leaders for English is to map out the texts in each year group. Pupils could be involved in selecting books to refresh the curriculum. The better the text, and the greater a teacher's love of it, the richer the learning experience.

2 "[Talk is] the most powerful tool of communication in the classroom and it's fundamentally central to the acts of teaching and learning" (Professor Frank Hardman in *The State of Speaking in Our Schools* by Will Millard and Loic Menzies, 2016). However, talk can be discouraged, rushed, unstructured or included as an afterthought. If pupils can't *say* good sentences, it's very unlikely they will *write* them. So, developing oracy in our classrooms and embedding it into our teaching sequences is essential. Visit **www.voice21.org** for a brilliant case study on the impact of teaching oracy.

3 Be a writer yourself – teachers who write teach writing better. Get involved in the brilliant Teachers as Writers project (**www.teachersaswriters.org**). Model writing to your pupils and let them see you writing when they are writing. Make writing ordinary to make their writing extraordinary: 'everyone's a writer in our classroom'.

4 Don't do all the thinking on behalf of pupils. It's *their* writing. Marking and feedback should prompt thinking, encourage pupils to consider their options and remind them to take ownership of the writing. Assessment shouldn't be a way for the teacher to totally control the outcomes, specifying exactly what each pupil should have in each piece. The W.R.I.T.E.R. sequence into which the following activities are organised contains many opportunities for the best kinds of formative assessment: pupils setting their own success criteria; peer assessment to discuss and evaluate writing choices; and editing based on self-assessment. These Assessment for Learning strategies will work more effectively if the learning intentions of each lesson are focused on skills, not outcomes. So, rather than telling the pupils 'We Are Learning To: Write a diary entry' or 'We Are Learning To: Write a letter' (both of these are outcomes), better that they are 'learning to organise their ideas into paragraphs'; to 'describie the positions of characters in a scene with prepositions' or to 'control the pace of a poem with punctuation'.

5 In addition to the teaching sequences you plan, ensure that your pupils are given time and space for free writing. This is the writer's equivalent of practising 'keepy-ups' at the park and is certain to help them to improve their skills. Liberate their thinking by leaving the free-writing unmarked. Perhaps once a term you could invite pupils to select one piece of free writing for you to mark.

6 Create a classroom environment which promotes independence and high expectations. Have displays, bookcases and tables full of support materials and prompts and expect the pupils to access these independently to think about and improve their writing. Display the pupils' best writing prominently to raise its profile. Most pupils are desperate to meet the expectations of their teacher – so it's vital that these expectations are high. One great idea I've come across is displaying every child's latest piece of writing on the wall. When a new one is complete, it is stapled on top. Over time, the pieces build up and pupils and parents love flicking through to see how much progress has been made.

7 Make links across the curriculum in your planning so that pupils transfer skills to deepen their learning. This means putting skills learnt in English to good use in other subjects, e.g. summarise your learning in this maths lesson in 20 words or fewer; develop your sentences about the water cycle using conjunctions and additional clauses; for your report, plan three paragraphs about your proudest achievements this year; or write up your forest school campfire menu using adverbials to add information. The links should go both ways, so that pupils bring knowledge and skills from across the curriculum into their English lessons, e.g. learning about the Antarctic in geography to add a sense of realism to a diary entry by one of Shackleton's crew; researching first-hand accounts of the Somme in History to inspire war poetry; attending an assembly led by a community group to support a debate about a local issue.

8 Lastly, plan to teach writing the 'right way round'. There is nothing more soul-destroying for pupils (or teachers) than to finish a piece of writing, only to have to look back and see the 'mistakes' identified by the teacher. Over time, pupils may get demoralised by this and start to see writing as a chore, or associate writing with failure. The W.R.I.T.E.R. sequence (p.8) looks forward, building up to a positive ending. It provides time for pupils to edit out mistakes themselves as the writing evolves, resulting in a higher quality, more positive and more motivating end for all concerned!

THE W.R.I.T.E.R. SEQUENCE

All the ideas work in their own right (I promise). However, if we are to achieve 'joined-up thinking', we need to construct sequences of lessons using the individual activities. There are 50 activities in this book, but teachers will no doubt have their own favourite activities which can be slotted in. The key principle is that the W.R.I.T.E.R. sequence is an effective structure by which to plan your lessons.

The stages of the sequence are not detached and should be seen as merging together. Although the sequence starts with 'Work on words', it would be ridiculous if pupils weren't working on words throughout the sequence. The same could be said of reading, talking, thinking and writing. These skills should be threads which run through the sequence and which are reinforced daily.

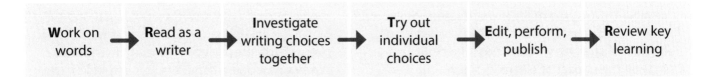

Work on words → **Read as a writer** → **Investigate writing choices together** → **Try out individual choices** → **Edit, perform, publish** → **Review key learning**

HOW THE STAGES WORK TOGETHER

	Purpose:	This is a good stage to:
Work on words	To introduce key words and ideas. To embed the teaching of spelling. To teach the context, the background, a sense of the real world, the history, the geography, the facts, etc. To ask the big questions, e.g. What would make people leave their homes? What makes a good pet? When was it most dangerous to speak your mind? What was life like in Roman times?	Reinforce and revise word skills, e.g. spelling. Start a new 'working wall', with a display of spellings which become 'non-negotiables'. Add key words to personal spelling lists. Model how to apply spelling strategies.
Read as a writer	To read texts which add a context to the learning. To explore and discuss good writers' choices. To learn new words and phrases. To expose the pupils to different writers, genres and periods. To inspire pupils to aspirational writing targets.	Continue to reinforce and revise word skills, e.g. dictionary skills. Consider possible success criteria for the writing to follow. Teach guided reading groups to address pupils' needs and any gaps in their prior learning. Model a range of reading skills from a reading toolkit. Display reading toolkit icons. Add ideas to the working wall.

Investigate writing choices together	For pupils to start considering the possible genre, audience and purpose of their own writing. To learn skills with the support of pairs and groups. To scaffold the first attempts. For pupils to practise the skills which may become success criteria later in the sequence.	Continue to reinforce and revise word skills, e.g. finding patterns in words. Select success criteria for our own writing. Model writing to the pupils. Facilitate shared writing in pairs and groups. Teach guided writing groups to address pupils' needs and any gaps in their prior learning. Embed the teaching or grammar, punctuation and spelling. Add ideas to the working wall.
Try out individual choices	For pupils to select the genre, audience and purpose for their own writing. To work more independently following the scaffolded first attempts. To experiment with individual writing choices which meet the success criteria. For pupils to plan the structure of their piece. For pupils to adopt different styles of writing for different purposes, e.g. level of formality, informative, descriptive, persuasive, extended narrative, etc. For pupils to think about cohesion and coherence – working out how they can get their ideas to work together. For pupils to 'have a go', make mistakes, and complete a draft version.	Continue to reinforce and revise word skills, e.g. thesaurus skills. Model how to select and reject different choices. Model planning to the pupils. Model writing cohesively to the pupils. Self and peer assess outcomes against the success criteria. Set the expectation that pupils complete a good draft. Mark and give feedback, ready for the pupil to respond by editing.
Edit, perform, publish	For pupils to re-read and re-work their draft. For pupils to respond to marking and feedback, focused on the success criteria. For pupils to edit their work for spelling and grammatical mistakes. For pupils to perform and/or publish to their audience. (A sense of audience will raise expectations and improve outcomes.) This could be a story circle, reading aloud, collating a collection of writing for a display, performing their poem, acting out their script, storytelling to younger years, presenting their work in assembly, etc.	Continue to reinforce and revise word skills, e.g. checking, identifying and learning from spelling mistakes. Self-assess by highlighting/annotating where the success criteria have been met. Model how to edit to the pupils. Identify remaining spelling mistakes. Write up 'in best'. Have fun with the outcomes.
Review key learning	To celebrate and share success. To reflect on and evaluate the writing outcomes. To review key learning and plan ahead.	To refer to the year group writing targets. To set new, personal writing targets.

Although its principles always remain the same, the sequence can be adapted according to the needs of the pupils, the situation, or the stage of the year. For example, a snappy version of the sequence works well in a 45–60 minute lesson or guided group: warm up with words; read and discuss an extract of rich text; model and share writing to get started; write independently, check that it's ready to read; read it out (all together or in pairs); review key learning.

Later in a school year, teachers could accelerate certain stages for some pupils (e.g. those expected to be working at Greater Depth), such as the Investigate writing choices together stage, because the pupils should be relying less on scaffolds, or the support of shared writing. For these pupils, a more direct progression from reading to writing may be more appropriate.

It can also be used successfully over a couple of lessons or a week, but I would recommend that the sequence is best used over two weeks. See the sample timetable at the bottom of this page.

Why two weeks? It's all to do with the shaded blocks. I have already highlighted some challenges faced by teachers – one being managing the content in the curriculum. A two-week sequence allows time to embed some of this content, and the resulting learning will complement and broaden the pupils' experience, drip-feeding a wide range of skills. Importantly, breaking up the sequence also provides pupils (and teachers) some variety, space and thinking time. Note, for example, the break between the **I** stage (completing a draft) and the **E** stage (editing and improving). This break allows the pupil to return to their work with fresh eyes, and they will inevitably notice things to improve when they do. As Zadie Smith advises budding writers: "Leave a decent space of time between writing something and editing it".

A few such sequences over the course of a school year is not only bound to produce a significant amount of writing but also plenty of useful evidence that the pupil can draft and edit, as well as contextual evidence of their spelling, grammar and punctuation skills.

As for the periods where you're not following a W.R.I.T.E.R. activity, the following tried-and-tested ideas are certain to enliven the learning in your classroom:

- Free writing
- Mindfulness (see **www.mindfulwriting.net**)
- Diary writing
- Poem of the week (you could read it every day for a week, then plan a lesson around it)
- Performance poetry
- Drama
- Reading comics/graphic novels
- Listening to an audio book
- Library visit/reading for pleasure
- Spelling games (see **www.mcmlearning.co.uk**)
- One-to-one targeted marking and feedback
- ICT room/immersive computer games
- Handwriting/calligraphy/art/printmaking/mapmaking.

EXAMPLE TIMETABLE

Monday	Tuesday	Wednesday	Thursday	Friday
W	W / R	R / i	I	

Monday	Tuesday	Wednesday	Thursday	Friday
I / T	T		E	RV

HOW TO USE THE ACTIVITIES

Imagine you are teaching a learning journey about differences, inspired by *The Boy in the Striped Pyjamas* by John Boyne as the whole-class text. Here is a potential sequence for this topic:

Stage of sequence	Pupils could:
W	Use Reading pictures 2 (W9) to discuss still and moving pictures of Auschwitz.
	Use Ready to research (W5) to investigate the historical context.
	Use Thinking dice (W2) to introduce and link key words, explore what pupils already know and add them to the working wall.
	Link the key words to a spelling pattern using, e.g. Prefix word webs (W8).
	(In geography) Draw a map labelled with key places, using words from the working wall.
R	(In history) Read a non-fiction text about Jewish deportation and transportation, using Annotation station (R5) to highlight key information.
	Group read key passages from *The Boy in the Striped Pyjamas* using Reading squad (R7).
	Close read a paragraph using Traffic light questions (R4).
	Explore a selection of John Boyne's sentences using Sentence knockout (R3).
I	Following the reading tasks, consider the children's own writing success criteria.
	In pairs, explore and practise grammar skills using the Grammatical sentences game (I6).
	Create some shared writing with a particular grammar focus after using, e.g. Cricket clauses (I11) or Time traveller (I7).
	Continue to read the text in different ways.
	Continue to explore and learn words.
T	Consider their writing choices and set writing success criteria using the Pre-launch checklist (T1).
	Choose a planning grid from Prepare to plan (T2) before planning their piece.
	Work on cohesion using Reference chains (T4).
	Draft their piece using Peruse before you choose (T5).
	(In art) Create their own picture or collage to present with their writing, an idea from Pre-launch checklist (T1).
	Continue to read the text in different ways.
	Continue to explore and learn words.
E	Edit and improve their draft using the Editing dice activity (E2).
	Edit spelling mistakes using Detect and correct (E3).
	Continue to read the text in different ways.
	Continue to explore and learn words.
R(V)	Update their personal writing targets using Target setter (RV2).
	Continue to read the text in different ways.
	Continue to explore and learn words.

AND FINALLY... THE ACTIVITIES

The pupil activity pages (odd-numbered pages) can be photocopied and used in your classroom straight away. The audience for the writing in the 50 activities is the pupil, the purpose being that teachers can adapt or copy the text to use in their own slides and resources.

The teacher pages provide practical tips and ways to adapt each activity. A common thread running through the teacher pages is the importance of the teacher modelling the skills required to the pupils.

You will notice that there are more activities towards the start of the sequence. This reflects the importance of the early stages of the sequence: get these right and good writing will surely follow.

The text and photos I have used will help to model each activity, but these can easily be replaced with extracts from different texts or images which relate to the class text or current learning journey. I hope you and your pupils enjoy the activities and that the W.R.I.T.E.R. sequence helps to support some brilliant writing!

Mark McCaughan
August 2017

NO PHOTOCOPIER?

No problem. Simply scan the QR code below with your smartphone or tablet to access digital copies of each of the pupil pages in this book.

Alternatively, the following link to register for access to the members' area of Mark's website:

https://goo.gl/jdqAYu

WORK ON WORDS

FUN WITH WORDS

In these activities, pupils flex their mental muscles by thinking about words in different ways. If we want them to write well, we need to start by building their confidence with words.

Pupils will learn:

- ☑ key vocabulary in context.
- ☑ how to be creative with words.
- ☑ how to approach words with confidence.
- ☑ to construct and deconstruct words.
- ☑ to think and talk about words.
- ☑ to enjoy words.

Preparation:

1 Download the pupil page or display one of the activities on the whiteboard.

2 Set a time limit.

3 At the end of the activity, ask the children to share some examples and review key learning.

Take it further!

- Create a bank of similar extension activities for pupils to access independently as part of their classroom routine.

- Set similar tasks for homework to engage parents.

- Have a fun with words activity on the working wall each week, for pupils to complete collaboratively as the week progresses.

Mark's notes

Having fun with words is very important – and a very good way for pupils to build their vocabulary. As P.D. James reminded us: "Increase your word power. Words are the raw material of our craft. The greater your vocabulary, the more effective your writing".

This type of activity is also a great way to ensure that there is always something interesting to think about when pupils enter the classroom. It helps to maximise learning time, settle the class and create a purposeful start (or end) to your lessons.

Regardless of their ability, all pupils will benefit from opportunities to paddle out of their cognitive comfort zone. Most importantly, though, this type of approach is vital for those disadvantaged pupils who are penalised in every aspect of their learning because they haven't encountered as many words and their various meanings as their peers. With regular exposure to activities like this, there is a chance that we can level the playing field for these pupils.

Visit **www.mcmlearning.co.uk** for loads of other ways to have fun with words.

FUN WITH WORDS ACTIVITY

PORTMANTEAU

A **portmanteau** is when you blend words together to make a new word, e.g. spork, Brexit or labradoodle. Can you invent some of your own?

A-Z LIST

Make an **A-Z list** in 10 minutes. What about: Things you could find on a beach; Happiness is…; New ice- cream flavours. Can you think of your own ideas?

WORD CHAIN

Make a chain of words, where the last letter of one word becomes the first letter of the next. To make it more challenging, stick to a theme, e.g. space: asteroid, debris, Saturn, Neptune, Earth, Haley's Comet, etc.

LIPOGRAM

A **lipogram** is a word game in which you write without using a particular letter.

(Original)

Mary had a little lamb,
Its fleece was white as snow,
And everywhere that Mary went,
The lamb was sure to go.

(Without A)

Polly owned the tiny sheep,
Its fleece glowed white like snow,
To every spot our Polly went,
The sheep would surely go.

Can you think of a poem or nursery rhyme to turn into a lipogram?

METAPHOR GAME

Complete the lines below and then think of other lines you could add:

If I were a colour, I would be…
If I were a football team, I would be…
If I were a smell, I would be…
If I were a bird, I would be…

You could also take the word 'be' off each line to add a twist.

KENNINGS

Kennings are descriptive phrases are from Old Norse, Icelandic and Anglo-Saxon poetry. They usually consist of two words, are often hyphenated, and are used to describe nouns, e.g. spear-din (battle), battle-sweat (blood), sleep of the sword (death), whale-road (sea). Some modern examples are salad-dodger and ankle-biter.

Can you invent some of your own?

HAIKU

A **haiku** is an unrhymed three-line poem. It is based on a traditional Japanese poetic form. The pattern of syllables looks like this:

Line 1: 5 syllables
Line 2: 7 syllables
Line 3: 5 syllables

Here's an example:

Whitecaps on the bay
A broken signboard banging
In the April wind.

Can you write your own?

DITLOIDS

These are **ditoids** – a type of word puzzle. Try to solve the clues below, the first one is done for you:

7 D of the W = 7 Days of the Week
12 M of the Y
26 L in the A
11 P in a F T
4 J in XF

Can you think of some to set your partner?

LETTERMORPHOSIS

What can you morph a word into by changing one letter at a time?

dog	love
log	live
lot	hive
cot	have
cat	hate

THINKING DICE

In this activity, pupils play a dice game based on key words and phrases; the game prompts them to make links between them.

Pupils will learn:

☑ key vocabulary in context.

☑ the meanings of words through talk.

☑ to link different areas of learning.

☑ how to spell key words.

☑ to listen well.

☑ how to use conjunctions and additional clauses to develop sentences.

☑ to write cohesively by developing links within sentences.

Preparation:

1 Photocopy the pupil page, enough for one between two, or display it on your interactive whiteboard.

2 Hand out the dice – one per group or pair.

Take it further!

- Set up a similar activity at the start of a lesson or unit to establish what the pupils already know.

- Set this as an assessment opportunity at the end of a lesson or unit.

- Create a thinking dice grid for topic themes, newspaper headlines or characters and events from a story or a poem.

Mark's notes

So often, pupils – even when they are taking GCSE and A Levels – miss out on higher marks because they fail to develop their answer. This activity plants the seeds of thinking that will help prevent this: What can I link this to? What else do I know that could strengthen my answer? How can I develop this point?

This activity allows the children to think and talk about the key words and the topic they relate to. Links to grammar might include conjunctions, relative clauses or simple, compound and complex sentences – but don't let the grammar strangle the thinking and talking! You could also use this activity as a scaffold for talk before pupils write their own grid of key words and phrases. Set a time limit or specify the number of rounds before the children get started.

THINKING DICE ACTIVITY

READ the words in the table below, which were copied from a class's working wall. **TALK** to your partner or group: What do you think the class was learning about? Why do you think that?

Now take it in turns to roll the thinking dice and discuss your answers together. For example, if you roll a 1, you could group St. Helens, Mount Etna and Hawaii as names of places, volcanoes or even geographical features higher than 2,000 metres. Over to you – see what you can think of!

earthquake	migration	Iceland	destruction	magma
Richter scale	Ring of Fire	pyroclastic flow	victims	plate
St. Helens	lava	hurricane	tsunami	fault
crust	boundary	Pacific	Hawaii	tremors
eruption	fertile soil	tornado	Mount Etna	Beaufort scale
landslide	population	San Francisco	buildings	epicentre

Dice	Action
•	**GROUP** three words together and explain the link between them.
••	**FIND** two words with differences.
•••	**FIND** two words with similarities.
••••	**DESCRIBE** something in ten words or fewer.
•••••	**DEFINE** the meaning of a word.
••••••	**NOTE DOWN** a word you need to learn more about.

THINK about your current learning – what are the key words and ideas for your topic?

WRITE your own table using the key words you thought of. This table can then be used for the thinking dice activity or as a word bank for your learning – so make sure you spell the key words correctly!

TOP TIP:

Use similar links and connections to make your writing more cohesive, e.g. When an earthquake triggered a landslide on Mount St. Helens in 1980, the resulting pyroclastic flow destroyed many buildings, and claimed 57 victims.

READING PICTURES 1

In this activity, pupils learn to think about describing the relationship between different things to their reader.

Pupils will learn:

☑ to understand prepositions and how they are used.

☑ to observe images carefully.

☑ key vocabulary in context.

☑ to think about their reader's needs.

Preparation:

1 Photocopy the pupil page, enough for one between two, or display it on your interactive whiteboard.

2 Be prepared to model a couple of examples to show pupils how you are thinking about the task and using prepositions.

3 Consider how pupils can source their own image following the shared example – a bank of magazine or newspaper images works well.

Take it further!

- Challenge pupils to make preposition phrases by adding other words before or after a preposition, e.g. Just around the corner from the station was the best sweet shop in town.

- Get pupils thinking about how prepositions can be used to 'zoom in' or 'zoom out'. Writers often use a triplet (three in a row) for this reason. Here's an example from *The Iron Woman* by Ted Hughes, which zooms the reader's attention down into the 'black water': "Today, as usual, the bridge was empty. As she crossed over it, she looked between the rails, into the black water."

- This activity also works well in any subject: to introduce a piece of art; to explore a key setting, e.g. a Victorian street scene; or to study a map. What about moving images: a clip of a volcano erupting; a scene from a film; a sequence from a wildlife documentary; or a key character or setting?

Mark's notes

One way to cope with this heavy content is the dreaded grammar worksheet – and I continue to see plenty of these in circulation. They have their place, of course: in the bin.

Much better to introduce an aspect of grammar in a more exploratory way so that the learning and outcomes aren't so predictable, limited and (dare I say) boring.

READING PICTURES 1 ACTIVITY

THINK about how good writers show their reader where the action is taking place. Using prepositions can be an effective way to achieve this, because these words can be used to make phrases which show the reader where things are positioned in relation to other things. This activity is an excellent way to practise prepositions and to observe the fine details in a scene which can bring your writing to life for your reader.

TALK with your partner about the photograph below. Take it in turns to describe the position of something in the image, using one of the prepositions suggested, e.g. *under* a hazy African sky, *beneath* soaring mountains, a mother elephant walks *towards* a waterhole. Keep going – see how many things you can spot and how these are positioned in relation to each other.

beneath

ahead

inside

past

above

outside

alongside

behind

opposite

beside

near

underneath

in

into

over

towards

beyond

through

Choose your own image but don't show your partner (yet). **WRITE** a description of the image using prepositions to show where things are in relation to one another.

READ the description to your partner while they draw what you are describing. Then, show them the picture and discuss how well you used prepositions to describe the position of things.

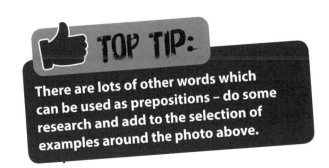

TOP TIP:

There are lots of other words which can be used as prepositions – do some research and add to the selection of examples around the photo above.

DICTIONARY SKILLS 1

In this activity, pupils learn how to use a dictionary so that, over time, it becomes a powerful weapon in their writing armoury.

Pupils will learn:

- ☑ alphabetical order.
- ☑ how to look up words.
- ☑ how to spell key words.
- ☑ to approach words with confidence.
- ☑ how to construct and deconstruct words.
- ☑ to read, think and talk about words.

Preparation:

1 Photocopy the pupil page, enough for one between two, or display it on your interactive whiteboard.

2 Ensure all pupils have a suitable dictionary with which they feel comfortable. This is vital because confidence can easily be knocked if the dictionary is too daunting.

Take it further!

- Provide a different dictionary for some pupils, particularly those with dyslexia. A spelling dictionary with an aural code is worth considering.

- Incorporate dictionary activities into your start-of-day routine, golden time or as part of a carousel.

- Set this activity as homework to engage parents.

Mark's notes

The Education Policy Institute's 2016 annual report confirmed that around 40 per cent of the gap between disadvantaged pupils and their peers is present at age five. An obvious feature of this gap is that disadvantaged pupils are likely to have a less-developed vocabulary. Unless we intervene effectively, the gap will never close.

Regular exposure to this type of activity is a great way to learn new words in the short term and to increase confidence with words in the long term. The activities themselves also make great settling activities, starters or tasks to make purposeful use of a few minutes here and there. They require a degree of independence, which means that all pupils will be on task, enabling the teacher to work with targeted pupils or groups.

DICTIONARY SKILLS 1 ACTIVITY

THINK – Did you know, there are up to three-quarters of a million words in the English language? And lots of these words come from French, Latin, Greek, Old Norse, Dutch, and many more. So, it's okay not to know them all, and it's certainly okay to look words up when you're not sure of their meaning or spelling.

READ the instructions to the activities below. These will help you to use dictionaries confidently – a very important skill for all writers to learn.

GUIDE WORDS

The words on the top of a dictionary page are called 'guide words'. These words list the first and last entries on the page.

Find an interesting word in your dictionary and fill in the blanks: _____

is found on the page between guide words _____ and _____.

The word means _____

_____.

Find another interesting word. Write a clue for your partner like this:

This word means _____

_____

and can be found between the guide words _____ and _____.

DICTIONARY EXPLORER

Choose one of your spellings. You have ten minutes to find out as much as you can about your word.

What is the plural?

Which parts of speech (word classes) can it be used as?

Are there other words in the same family?

How many meanings does it have?

How many syllables are in it?

What are its origins?

 **TOP TIP:**

Don't wait for your teacher to prompt you to use a dictionary! Have one to hand when you read and write so that you can understand the meaning and effect of words – this will help you to make the best word choices.

CROSSWORD CLUES – IN PAIRS OR GROUPS

Flick through the dictionary to select words about which you can write great clues. Clues could be written like this:

A multi-legged creature (9 letters, page 132)

The opposite of _____ (5 letters, page 132)

Don't go snorkelling with this apex predator (8 letters, page 146)

Swap clues with your group or partner and get solving!

READY TO RESEARCH

In these activities, pupils consider and collect the information they need to bring a piece of writing to life for the reader. This may be the key events which will make up a biography, the most significant facts for an historical account or scientific facts to strengthen a report.

Pupils will learn:

☑ research skills.

☑ how to access information in different types of texts.

☑ how to think about their reader's needs.

☑ subject and general knowledge.

☑ how to plan a cohesive and coherent whole text.

Preparation:

1 Model how to research a topic, how to use an index, how to skim and scan for information, how to make notes, and how to refer to these when you are writing.

2 Visit **www.mcmlearning.co.uk** to find several ideas which will get your pupils thinking about the activities on the pupil page.

Take it further!

- Set tasks which require independent research, e.g. My sporting hero; My dream holiday destination; or a biography of a real or fictional character.

- Ask different groups to research different aspects of a topic and be ready to share their learning.

- Assess the research task itself and ask pupils to set their own criteria for what makes effective research. This might be: clear, concise notes; relevant, interesting content; or being able to present the information to the class.

- Use the completed research to teach cohesive devices, e.g. Which of my findings will make the best paragraphs? What patterns of words do I want to use once I start writing? Could I put these two ideas together in one compound or complex sentence?

Mark's notes

Another consequence of the heavy content in the curriculum is that we could be inclined to teach at such a rate of knots that we neglect some good-old-fashioned thinking time. This could result in pupils becoming dependent on 'spoon feeding' and it's important to expect pupils to think independently. It's amazing how much impact some independent research can have on a pupil's final writing outcome, especially in terms of the flow of the writing and the coherence of the whole text.

Most importantly, though, using this type of activity early in the sequence helps pupils to learn the context of a piece of writing. Recently, I worked with a teacher in Hastings who'd planned a great unit about smugglers. He had identified an obvious barrier to progress: some of his class in this seaside town had never even been to the beach. If we don't teach the context of a piece of writing, the disadvantaged pupils are the most disadvantaged.

READY TO RESEARCH ACTIVITY

"By failing to prepare, you are preparing to fail," said Benjamin Franklin, one of the founding fathers of the USA. Think about it – why do you think Luke Skywalker did all that 'use the Force' practice in the swamp with Yoda before his lightsabre battle with (spoiler alert) his dad? (That must have been awkward at tea-time!)

READ and **THINK** about the two pieces of homework below. **TALK** to your partner about the texts – which pupil has researched the topic well? How do you know?

WINDOW WILDLIFE WATCH HOMEWORK EXAMPLE 1

I looked out of the window a couple of times and saw a bird. It could fly. Then Mum called me for tea. It was chips. When I had finished, the bird was gone but a large red animal (I don't think it was a bird) with a bushy tail was leaving a 'little message' on the lawn!

WINDOW WILDLIFE WATCH HOMEWORK EXAMPLE 2

I set up my own 'hide' on the window ledge and waited. It didn't take long for me to spot 'Britain's favourite bird', the robin. This red-breasted, year-round resident of the UK's hedgerows, parks and gardens is often heard before seen, but here he was in our garden, perched on a branch of the holly bush. Perhaps he was looking for seeds or insects in the bush, but then swooped down to the lawn, pecking the soil for a tasty worm.

To add some life to your writing, it's important to research the topic and start organising your ideas. **READ** the research radial below, and **THINK** about how it helped to build example 2.

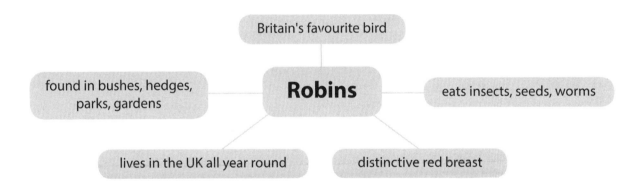

ASK YOURSELF:

What's the topic I'm researching? Where can I look for information? What research questions can I ask to help me? (See below.) What are the most interesting points for my reader? Which key words and phrases can I use in my writing?

I keep six honest serving-men

(They taught me all I knew);

Their names are **What** and **Why** and **When**

And **How** and **Where** and **Who**. (Rudyard Kipling)

Use Kipling's question words to ask yourself some questions about the topic you're researching.

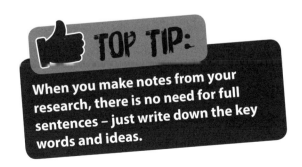

TOP TIP:

When you make notes from your research, there is no need for full sentences – just write down the key words and ideas.

MAGIC WORDS

In this activity, pupils take a word and think about the different ways it can be used.

Pupils will learn:

- ☑ how to explore the meanings of words through talk.
- ☑ how to construct and deconstruct words.
- ☑ that words can be used in different ways for different effects.
- ☑ about prefixes and suffixes.
- ☑ how to understand aspects of grammar, e.g. compound words and the eight word classes.

Preparation:

1 Photocopy the pupil page, enough for one between two, or display it on your interactive whiteboard.

2 Model a couple of examples to show pupils how you are thinking about the task and how you can manipulate the meaning and use of a word.

Take it further!

- Isolate an aspect of language, e.g. suffixes, and teach how these can be used to change tense.
- Set this task as homework to engage parents.
- Use some key words from the learning journey – once these have been explored, they can be displayed for pupils to refer to.
- Use a word from Modern Foreign Languages.

Mark's notes

The largely pointless KS2 spelling, grammar and punctuation test seems to reward shallow learning about what different aspects of language are called, or how one particular form of a word is spelt. However, deep and meaningful learning can only be achieved if pupils learn a more flexible approach to words and their many nuances. By helping them to learn in this way, we are giving them a chance to apply this flexible thinking to their writing. We can drill pupils to identify the progressive form of verbs in a test, but doesn't it make more sense to train them to be able to work out when this choice might be the best choice?

Details of how to order more resources like this one can be found online at **www.mcmlearning.co.uk**. These work best printed onto A3 and laminated for repeat use.

MAGIC WORDS ACTIVITY

READ the words in the boxes below. **THINK** about the meaning of the words and **TALK** to your partner about them. Look up any words you're not sure of. Think about how words can be used in different ways for different effects. Consider the word 'magic' – although it is normally used as a noun, we could 'magic' it into an adverb (magically), an adjective (magical), a phrase (black magic), or transform it into another noun (magician) by changing the suffix.

Select a word from your reading book and **WRITE** it in the box beneath the magician's hat. Become a word magician and see what you can turn it into. It won't be possible to fill very box for every word.

a word which can be used as a verb?	Can you turn _____ into…	a phrase?
a word which can be used as a noun?		a different word by adding a prefix?
a word which can be used as an adverb?		a different word by adding a suffix?
a word which can be used as an adjective?	a compound word?	a shorter word?

TOP TIP:

There are 8 word classes (or parts of speech): verbs, adverbs, conjunctions, nouns, determiners, adjectives, prepositions and pronouns. However, it's best not to think about a word by its word class, e.g. 'it's a noun'. Word classes are flexible and words can usually be made to work in different ways. It's best to ask, 'how is the word working in this sentence?' Look at these examples: A fast runner won the race. ('Fast' is used as an adjective to describe a noun.)

She ran fast. ('Fast' is used an adverb to modify a verb.)

After the operation, the patient had to fast for 24 hours. ('Fast' is used as a verb.)

The patient's fast lasted 24 hours. ('Fast' is used as a noun.)

WORD SPLASH

In this activity, pupils take a word and think about the different ways it can be used.

Pupils will learn:

☑ aspects of grammar and language, e.g. synonyms, etymology, morphology.

☑ to read, think and talk about words.

☑ to work collaboratively.

☑ to approach words with confidence.

☑ how to construct and deconstruct words.

Preparation:

1 Photocopy the pupil page, enough for one between two, or display it on your interactive whiteboard.

2 Model a couple of examples to show pupils how you are thinking about the task and scoring points. Importantly, model that it might not be possible to fill every box, and the resilience required not to get 'stuck'.

Details of how to order a complete set of similar resources called Thinking Spelling can be found at **www.mcmlearning.co.uk**. These work best printed onto A3 and laminated for repeat use.

Take it further!

• Use a word from Modern Foreign Languages.

• Use some key words from the learning journey – once these have been explored, they can be displayed for pupils to refer to.

Mark's notes

You'll notice the emphasis I've placed on modelling throughout the book. I think this is the best way to empower pupils to think as writers. By modelling, you can teach them that it's okay to change your mind, cross something out, get something wrong, be unsure about the spelling of a word, etc.

About the word 'cross', for example, you could say, 'Let's have a go with a simple sentence about a (completely fictional) teacher: *The teacher was cross*. It's a simple sentence because it's only got one clause. It's also a statement.'

Choosing to use an antonym
'How could we keep the same idea but with an antonym? *'Calm' was not a word one could use to describe Miss Bull during maths last Wednesday.*'

Choosing to write the sentence as a question
'How about a question? These are a great way to interest the reader. *Why was Miss Bull so cross? Surely it could have nothing to do with Kevin practising his fractions by cutting Lottie's pigtails into quarters.* I'm going to mark 'practising' to check later because sometimes I get that one wrong.'

Choosing to build phrases
'*The long-suffering teacher, who now glared at Kevin, was becoming very cross.* Very cross is a phrase just like cross, but it sounds stronger.'

This is not shared writing because the pupils aren't involved – they are just watching and listening. This type of activity will generate unexpected and rich outcomes, so there will be plenty of learning to share as a class.

WORD SPLASH ACTIVITY

READ the words in the boxes below. **THINK** about the meaning of the words and **TALK** to your partner about them. Look up any words you're still not sure of. Together, select a word to 'splash' – this could be a topic word, a word you've been struggling to spell, or just a word you find interesting.

Can you think of a word with the same meaning (a synonym)?

(2 POINTS)

Can you think of a word with the opposite meaning (an antonym)?

(2 POINTS)

Can you think of a word it rhymes with?

(2 POINTS)

Can you make a phrase using the word?

(2 POINTS)

What is the word's root word?

(2 POINTS)

The word is:

Can you add a suffix to change the tense of the word?

(3 POINTS)

What does the word mean?

(5 POINTS)

Can you add a prefix to change the word?

(3 POINTS)

Are there any shorter words within the word?

(2 POINTS)

Can you write a statement containing the word?

Can you write a question containing the word?

(4 POINTS EACH)

How can this word be used in a sentence (as an adjective, as a noun, etc.)?

(2 POINTS)

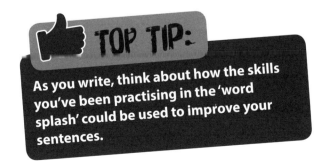

TOP TIP: As you write, think about how the skills you've been practising in the 'word splash' could be used to improve your sentences.

Igniting Children's Writing © Mark McCaughan, 2018

PREFIX WORD WEBS

In this activity, pupils choose a prefix and create their own word web to explore the meaning of the prefix.

Pupils will learn:

☑ how to spell key words.

☑ to approach words with confidence.

☑ how to construct and deconstruct words.

☑ how to find patterns of spelling and meaning between different

Preparation:

1 Photocopy the pupil page, enough for one between two, or display it on your interactive whiteboard.

2 Model an example to show pupils how you are thinking about prefixes and their meanings.

Take it further!

- Make some prefix cards and meaning cards for pupils to match in pairs.

- Use different questioning techniques over time to embed the learning, e.g.

  - How could we change the meaning of this word by adding a prefix?

  - Why is a circus called a circus and how do you know?

  - Does the prefix 'bio-' mean: a. washing powder; b. life; c. light?

  - Which groups could you put these prefixes into?

  - Write a true or false quiz about prefixes to test your partner.

- As homework, ask the children to find film titles which contain a prefix, e.g. *Batman Returns*, *Unforgiven*, *Transformers*.

Mark's notes

By learning prefixes, pupils will start to break words down into their component parts. In time, they'll have a better chance of avoiding common spelling mistakes like the classic 'dissappear' because they'll think about attaching 'dis-' (not diss) to the root word 'appear', just like they would for 'dislike', 'discount' or 'disappoint'.

Perhaps more significantly, this type of activity allows pupils to explore the meaning of the prefixes, and they will soon start noticing patterns: how 'dis-' plays a similar role to 'un-'; how 'di-', 'tri-', 'bi-', 'quad-', etc. describe number; how 'therm-' seems to create a pattern of words about heat.

Around the country, countless hours are spent on spelling tests in our classrooms. Might this type of activity be a better use of time?

At the equally important, other end of words are suffixes, and a similar activity called Super Suffixes can be downloaded from the Spelling downloads section of **www.mcmlearning.co.uk**.

PREFIX WORD WEBS ACTIVITY

A prefix is a group of letters you can add to the beginning of a root word. **TALK** to your partner about examples of prefixes and how they change the meaning of words they are added to. **THINK** about how a prefix changes the meaning of these words.

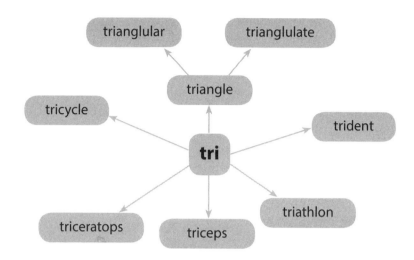

triangular   trianglulate

triangle

tricycle   trident

tri

triceratops   triceps   triathlon

READ the prefixes below and think about where you may have seen them before. Above is an example of a word web for the prefix 'tri'. This can help you work out a pattern of meaning – 'tri' means three.

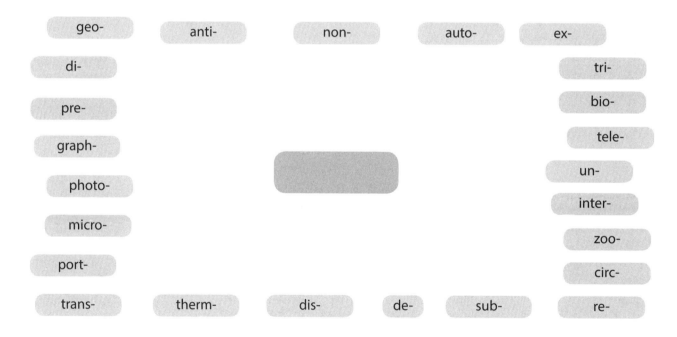

geo-   anti-   non-   auto-   ex-

di-   tri-

pre-   bio-

graph-   tele-

photo-   un-

micro-   inter-

port-   zoo-

circ-

trans-   therm-   dis-   de-   sub-   re-

Choose a prefix from the list above, or another example you can think of, and **WRITE** your own word web to help you work out the meaning of the prefix. What patterns of meaning can you find?

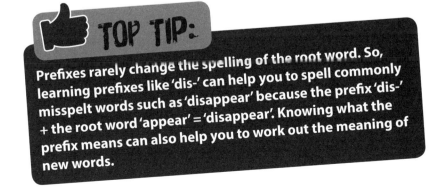

TOP TIP:

Prefixes rarely change the spelling of the root word. So, learning prefixes like 'dis-' can help you to spell commonly misspelt words such as 'disappear' because the prefix 'dis-' + the root word 'appear' = 'disappear'. Knowing what the prefix means can also help you to work out the meaning of new words.

READING PICTURES 2

In this activity, pupils apply a wide range of reading skills to a still image.

Pupils will learn:

☑ the context of a scene or a situation.

☑ a range of reading skills.

☑ how to ask and answer questions.

☑ to work collaboratively.

☑ how to listen and take notes.

Preparation:

1 Photocopy the pupil page, enough for one between two, or display it on your interactive whiteboard.

2 Consider the best way to group pupils – mixed ability is recommended.

3 Establish some ground rules for the talk. This is an important stage to ensure that everyone is comfortable, engaged and knows that the expectations are high.

How about downloading my Talk Dial at **www.mcmlearning.co.uk** to help with this?

Take it further!

• Use a cartoon or portrait instead of a painting or scene.

• Edit the questions to use this activity with a text – most of the questions will work well if you change 'artist' to 'writer'.

Mark's notes

This activity is a good way to teach pupils that their writing is just like drawing or painting: it will have an audience and the writing choices they make will affect this audience.

There is no shortage of stunning picture or illustrated books to complement a class novel or learning journey. If you are in need of inspiration, a good starting point is The CILIP Kate Greenaway Medal (**www.carnegiegreenaway.org.uk/ greenaway.php**).

READING PICTURES 2 ACTIVITY

It can help to **THINK** about the choices an artist has made before you think about your own choices as a writer. Select a painting or illustration related to a book, topic or theme you're going to write about. Form a group of three and number yourselves 1, 2 and 3. Your roles are:

Number	Role	Instructions
1	Picture reader	When you are asked a question, 'read' the image before you answer.
2	Questioner	Read questions from the table below to the picture reader. When you are only given the start of the question, think of the best way to complete it. After three questions, change roles.
3	Note-taker	Listen to the conversation between the reader and the questioner. Note down any interesting words and phrases which might help with your writing later.

Here are the questions:

1 When you look at the picture, how do your eyes travel across the page?

2 Is there anything in the picture you have seen in real life?

3 Is there anything in the picture you're not sure of?

4 What do you call…?

5 What do you notice about the background?

6 What do you notice about the foreground?

7 What do you notice about…?

8 What do you think about…?

9 Is there anything in the picture that you didn't notice straight away?

10 What feelings or emotions might the image produce?

11 Tell me something about…

12 How has the artist created a sense of…?

13 Why do you think the artist has chosen to…?

14 What question would you like to ask the artist?

15 What is the significance of…?

16 Can you find a similarity and a difference?

17 In your opinion, what is the artist's best choice?

18 If you could, what would you change about the picture?

 **TOP TIP:**

Before you write, read the notes; there may be some interesting words and phrases for you to use. As you write, think about your own choices and how you want to affect your reader – it's like being an artist, but using words instead of paint!

Igniting Children's Writing © Mark McCaughan, 2018

ALPHABET SCRAMBLE

In this activity, pupils compete to get to the end of the alphabet by thinking of examples of different types of words, such as proper nouns, verbs and compound words.

Pupils will learn:

☑ alphabetical order.

☑ how to spell an increasingly broad range of words.

☑ new vocabulary by listening to the responses of others.

☑ how to explore the meanings of words through talk.

☑ aspects of grammar.

Preparation:

1 Photocopy the pupil page, enough for one per group.

2 You will need two dice per group, counters for each player and something for the pupils to write on.

3 Limit the length of time the pupils are allowed to spend thinking of an answer to their dice roll. How long this is depends on the ability of your group.

Details of how to order a complete set of my Thinking Spelling resources can be found at **www.mcmlearning.co.uk**. These work best printed onto A3 and laminated for repeat use.

Take it further!

• Use this as an end-of-day whole-class race, with pupils in teams.

Mark's notes

You could start the class off with a heads and tails activity, like the one below:

verbs	usually modify verbs, but can also modify adjectives, prepositions, other adverbs or a whole sentence.
nouns	are words from other languages which have become commonly used in English, e.g. bungalow, vanilla, kindergarten.
prepositions	are *doing, being* or *having* words.
adjectives	are made when two words combine to make one word, e.g. playground, elsewhere, sunflower.
adverbs	are words that describe a noun.
proper nouns	are words that give the name of some specific thing or set of things.
foreign words	are words, starting with a capital letter, which give us the actual name of the person, place, thing, or idea.
compound words	show the relationship between parts of a sentence and are usually followed by a noun phrase.

ALPHABET SCRAMBLE ACTIVITY

To warm up, **THiNK** about these words and **TALK** to your partner about what they mean:

verb	noun	preposition	adjective

proper noun	adverb	foreign word	compound word

Choose an opponent (or opponents) and play 'alphabet scramble', a fun way to practise using all these different types of words.

It's simply a race from A to Z. Place your markers on the start line and roll the dice to see who goes first. Take it in turns to roll the dice and move your counter along the alphabet. Each time you land on a letter, roll the dice again to decide your spelling challenge. The challenges are:

Dice total	Challenge		Dice total	Challenge
2	Spell a verb starting with your letter		8	Spell a foreign word starting with your letter
3	Spell a noun starting with your letter		9	Spell a compound word starting with your letter
4	Spell a preposition starting with your letter		10	Spell a verb starting with your letter
5	Spell an adjective starting with your letter		11	Spell an adjective starting with your letter
6	Spell an adverb starting with your letter		12	Spell a preposition starting with your letter
7	Spell a proper noun starting with your letter			

If you write down a correct answer within the time limit, your marker remains where it is. If you are unsuccessful, move 2 spaces back. The first player to the finish wins!

START

A → B → C → D → E → F → G → H → I → J

T ← S ← R ← Q ← P ← O ← N ← M ← L ← K

U → V → W

Z ← Y ← X

FINISH

TOP TIP:
Have a dictionary handy because answers should be spelt correctly!

DICTIONARY SKILLS 2

In this activity, pupils continue to learn how to use a dictionary in different ways, so that, over time, they become increasingly confident.

Pupils will learn:

☑ alphabetical order.

☑ how to look up words.

☑ how to spell key words.

☑ to approach words with confidence.

☑ how to construct and deconstruct words.

☑ to read, think and talk about words.

Preparation:

1 Photocopy the pupil page, enough for one between two, or display it on your interactive whiteboard.

2 Ensure all pupils have a suitable dictionary with which they feel comfortable. This is vital because confidence can easily be knocked if the dictionary is too daunting.

Details of how to order a complete set of my Thinking Spelling resources can be found at **www.mcmlearning.co.uk**. These work best printed onto A3 and laminated for repeat use.

Take it further!

• For some pupils, particularly those with dyslexia, a spelling dictionary with an aural code is worth considering.

• Incorporate dictionary activities into your start-of-day routine, golden time or as part of a carousel.

• Set something like this as homework to engage parents.

Mark's notes

I loved my junior school – though it seems a long time ago now! However, with the benefit of hindsight, I've come to realise that some of the teaching wasn't exactly cutting edge. One teacher would sit sharpening pupils' pencils with his pen knife for hours on end. Another would put three titles on the board and then we'd choose one and paint for several hours without bothering him as he mulled over his betting slip. Another hooked me with Roald Dahl's *Danny the Champion of the World*, then refused to keep reading it because she was finding it 'boring'.

On the plus side, I always seemed to be on task, and I did okay – but I wonder how the kids who didn't read at home or get taken to the library fared.

We also did hundreds of alphabetical-order tasks, and using a dictionary regularly definitely made me more confident with words. The Dictionary Skills 2 activities are great for independent learning and to encourage the pupils to have fun with words, from setting each other puzzles to making up silly stories. These activities prepare the children for the spelling test, while instilling them with a broader understanding of spelling and grammar (and without boring them to death).

DICTIONARY SKILLS 2 ACTIVITY

THINK – did you know that there are three-quarters of a million words in the English language more than there were a week ago? In fact, the number grows all the time. In 2016, the Oxford English Dictionary added over 1000 new words, including 'glamping', 'bovver' and 'deffo'. Am I bovvered? Deffo – practising your dictionary skills should be a top priority!

READ the instructions to the activities below. These will help you to use dictionaries confidently which is a very important skill for all writers to learn.

DICTIONARY MULTI-CHOICE

Each player selects an interesting word from the dictionary and writes a question with three possible answers. Players then take it in turns to solve each other's questions. Here are a few to get you started:

Is an iguana a bird, a lizard or a tree?

Is enoki a fish, an asteroid or a Japanese mushroom?

Is a pomegranate a rock, a fruit or a weapon?

Does the verb to befuddle mean to confuse, to search or to cuddle?

If you are disgruntled are you hungry, disappointed or smelly?

DICTIONARY FIBBER

You will need a slip of paper for each player. Some of the slips have 'true' written on them and some have 'false'. At the start of each round, hand the slips out face down. Each player secretly selects an interesting and unusual word from the dictionary. The 'true' players copy down the correct meaning of their word from the dictionary. The other players invent or copy a 'false' meaning (but should still pretend to be looking closely at their dictionary). Players take it in turns to state their word and read out the meaning they have written. Other players decide whether the meaning is 'true' or 'false'.

DICTIONARY STORY GAME

Once upon a time there was a story game. The story was created around a group, with players taking turns. The first player began the story but left their idea unfinished. She said 'It all started near a...'

Excitedly, the second player flicked to a page in the dictionary, and skimmed around the page to find a word which added to the story. She said, 'It all started near a **forest**'. This player then developed the story for the next player by adding, 'where there lived a...'

Not wanting to be left out, the next player took over in the same way and continued, 'It all started near a **forest**, where there lived a **sausage**. The sausage was...'

Now have a go in your group – how long can you keep the story going?

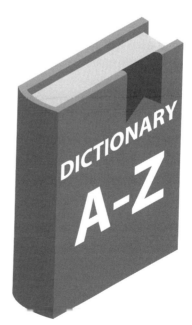

TOP TIP:

Having fun with your words is very important.

SNAKES AND LADDERS VOCABULARY GAME

In this activity, pupils play a board game in which they progress around the board by replacing certain 'over-used' words with another word.

Pupils will learn:

☑ to read, think and talk about words.

☑ new vocabulary by listening to the responses of others.

☑ how to explore the meanings of words through talk.

☑ to make the best choice of vocabulary with the reader in mind.

Preparation:

1 Photocopy the activity sheet, enough for one between two.

2 You will need two dice per group and counters for each player.

3 Consider the best way to group pupils – mixed ability is recommended.

Take it further!

- Play the game with a thesaurus to help pupils. However, it's important for them to think about alternative words and phrases they might already know before they turn to the thesaurus.

- Create your own class thesaurus with a different page for each of the words in red. Think about other pages you could add – how about pages for colours, e.g. blue, green? How about feelings, e.g. happy, scared? How about verbs, e.g. to say? Which other pages could you all create to help you with your writing? Over time, this could become a powerful resource in the classroom routine.

Mark's notes

Be careful how you pitch this activity because pupils need to understand that writing can be spoilt by over-elaborate vocabulary choice which spirals out of control – this is often a limiting factor when pupils fall short of Greater Depth Standard, hence the comments on the pupil page regarding the word 'said'. Pupils should be encouraged to change words for better words, or none at all. That said, this is a good activity for encouraging pupils to develop a broader vocabulary to choose from.

SNAKES AND LADDERS VOCABULARY GAME ACTIVITY

THINK about words that are commonly used in what you read. Sometimes, this is a deliberate choice by the writer. For example, some very successful writers only ever use 'said' in their reporting clauses. However, repeating certain words can become tiresome for the reader, so this activity will get you to think about mixing up your word choices.

You will need a dice and at least two players. Take turns to roll the dice. If you land at the base of a ladder, climb it, but if you land on the tail of a snake, you must slide down it.

Once you've landed on a square, roll the dice again to determine how many alternatives for the underlined word(s) you need to say to your playing partner(s), e.g. if you land on square 18 and then roll a 3, you need to think of three synonyms for 'happy'. This could be a single word or a phrase. If you are successful, move ahead two squares. If you are unsuccessful, move back two squares. The first player to the finish wins.

FINISH

24 Charlie <u>walked</u> towards the sea.

23 The caterpillar <u>moved</u> along the leaf.

22 The weary <u>old</u> lady <u>sat</u> on the park bench.

21 "I need to tell you a dangerous secret," <u>said</u> Millie.

20 A lone wolf <u>looked</u> across the frozen pond.

19 The cake was <u>nice</u>.

13 Losing the key was a <u>big</u> problem.

14 Dan was <u>quite</u> surprised when his spade hit metal.

15 In the cockpit, the pilot was <u>really</u> hot.

16 "This cream cake is <u>very</u> tasty," said Ella.

17 In the aftermath of the battle, the Captain could see <u>lots</u> of casualties.

18 The puppy was <u>happy</u> to see its owner.

12 Lizzie was <u>sad</u> to say goodbye to her teacher.

11 "I <u>like</u> my new bike," said Mo.

10 A <u>bad</u> king ruled the vast nation.

9 <u>Suddenly</u>, a great roar interrupted the silence.

8 Look at the <u>amazing</u> colours of the bird's feathers.

7 A <u>beautiful</u> princess stepped out of the carriage.

START

1 Billy is <u>good</u> at cricket but he is <u>amazing</u> at tennis.

2 The end of term party was great <u>fun</u>.

3 Freshly baked bread is delicious to <u>eat</u>.

4 Dad <u>lay</u> on the sofa watching the golf.

5 The startled rabbit <u>ran</u> into the undergrowth.

6 "Keep your head down," <u>said</u> the escaped prisoner.

TOP TIP:

Any of the underlined words above could be the best word choice in a particular sentence. Sometimes, a simple choice is best. However, as you write, consider the best words possible for the effect you want to create. Think about the change in: 'Keep your head down,' said/pleaded/whispered the escaped prisoner. How would each different word choice affect the reader, and which one would you choose?

READING PICTURES 3

In this activity, pupils describe an image using notes and observations they have made about it.

Pupils will learn:

☑ key vocabulary in context.

☑ how to take notes.

☑ about aspects of grammar, e.g. phrases.

☑ to ask questions about their learning.

☑ to observe, record and select details from an image.

Preparation:

1 Photocopy the pupil page, enough for one each, or display it on your interactive whiteboard.

2 Model an example to show pupils how you are thinking about the task and making notes around an image.

3 Pupils will need access to images, so scheduling some time in the library might work well.

Take it further!

- Provide some words in each box as a starting point or scaffold.

- Assign a box to different members of a group, who should then collaborate on some shared writing on poster paper, ready to feed back to the rest of the class.

Mark's notes

If, like in the example, we are expecting pupils to write about an event from the past, we need to give them a chance to experience how things looked, sounded and felt. We can build the sense of context further through film clips, sound files, assemblies, visiting experts or music from the time. Your local library service may also have artefacts that can be borrowed, and there may be a local place to visit to enrich the learning. I know, for example, that pupils who have actually worn a steel helmet at Newhaven Fort will empathise with the soldiers in the picture.

As a good way to stretch the more able, note the reference to abstract ideas – things that aren't in the image. By getting pupils to deepen their thinking like this, they will start to develop an understanding of the power of what is left unsaid, is only hinted at or inferred – these are all good skills for producing work of Greater Depth Standard.

READING PICTURES 3 ACTIVITY

THINK about how being observant can help you to describe interesting details for your reader.

TALK to your partner about a scene you are going to describe. This could be an historical photograph, an illustration, a painting or something you've drawn yourself. Around the picture, make notes and observations like in the example below, taken from a learning journey about World War One.

WHEN?

WORDS
wartime

PHRASES
World War One
The Great War
1914-18
July 1916
100 years ago

WHERE?

WORDS
France

PHRASES
The Somme
The Western Front
in the trenches
on the frontline

WHAT'S IN THE PICTURE?

WORDS
trench
helmets
explosions
uniform
soil
sign

PHRASES
soldiers waiting to go over the top
troops huddled together
taking cover
featureless landscape
dirty, khaki uniform
cramped conditions
a lonely sign
a shattered tree

WHAT'S THERE THAT CAN'T BE SEEN?

WORDS
fear
shellfire
memories
gas?
companionship

PHRASES
the advancing enemy
memories of home
fear of going over the top
all in it together
photographs of loved ones

QUESTIONS TO RESEARCH
Why did the armies dig trenches?
How far away were the enemy?
What did the soldiers eat?
How long would they stay in a trench?
What started the war?

READ the notes you have made about your scene. Are there any ideas which would work well together? Which idea would be the best to start with? Which would make a good ending? Are there any you want to get rid of?

WRITE the scene and then read it to your partner. Think about how making your notes helped you to write well.

 **TOP TIP:**

You don't have to use every single idea in your writing. As you write, select the ideas which work best and that your reader will find most interesting.

Igniting Children's Writing © Mark McCaughan, 2018

R

READ AS A WRITER

READING CHALLENGE

In this activity, pupils challenge themselves to broaden their reading experiences.

Pupils will learn:

- ☑ to apply their reading skills to a wide range of texts.
- ☑ how to find ideas and inspiration for their writing by reading good writers.
- ☑ how to be open to new ideas, from sources they may not have thought to read.
- ☑ to be resilient when faced with an unfamiliar text.

Preparation:

1 Photocopy the pupil page, enough for one each. This could be pasted into the pupil's book or reading journal. Alternatively, you could display it on your interactive whiteboard.

2 Ensure that your pupils have access to the best selection of books your budget can provide. Strengthen your links to the library service, visit the school library regularly and engage parents to ensure that the children are always reading something good.

Take it further!

- Leave some blank squares to allow pupils to add their own entries.
- Track progress as the year continues. This is a good opportunity for links to maths, e.g. by analysing the data gathered; displaying the data in graphs and charts.
- Link the challenge to World Book Day; ask members of staff to read from books they loved when they were younger.

Mark's notes

Here we move on to a selection of activities which will support pupils to read as a writer. If there is an irreplaceable stage of the W.R.I.T.E.R. sequence, it's this one – the reading. And if pupils are immersed in the right reading culture, their writing will inevitably improve 'by osmosis'.

This task is unashamedly challenging and is intended to help prise some pupils away from their device screens – a national epidemic in my humble opinion.

I believe that the way to accelerate progress in reading is to raise the level of challenge rather than reduce it. If we don't stretch the pupils, they will soon associate their reading experiences with a demoralising knock to their self-esteem. So, expect them to join in with reading tasks around rich texts of all kinds: a paragraph from a Booker prize winner; an article from a quality Sunday newspaper; a scene by Shakespeare. The teachers I have worked with who have taught from a challenging whole-class text (*Ghost Hawk* by Susan Cooper springs to mind) are often astonished at the leap in progress their pupils make.

This activity models those high expectations to the pupils, and it would be very powerful for them to see that the teacher has his or her own reading challenge going on.

READING CHALLENGE ACTIVITY

Here's something to **THINK** about: if you want to be a good writer, there is nothing more important than being a good reader. And the best way to be a good reader is to read lots of different texts written by lots of different writers. What a lot of lots!

TALK to your partner about how many of these you have read in the past 12 months:

a newspaper article	a leaflet, advert or flyer	a detective story	subtitles on a foreign film	a biography or autobiography
a book by your favourite author	something set in the future	a non-fiction book	a menu	a picture book or graphic novel
a book about animals/sport/science/history/art/music/food	a book by a writer you'd never heard of	a book written by a Children's Laureate	a science fiction story	a myth, legend or fantasy story
an obituary	a poem	a book you loved when you were younger	a recipe	lyrics from a song
a book recommended by a friend	a funny book	an adventure story	a sports report	a travel guide
a set of instructions	a film or theatre review	a blog	an article on a website	a short story
a scene from a TV, play or film script	a book review	a Carnegie Greenaway prize winner	something written by a friend	a comic

Challenge yourself! Select and circle 10 text types you have *not* read in the past 12 months from the table above. Over time, find good examples of the 10 text types you have selected and enjoy reading them.

TOP TIP:

When you read something by a writer you like, try to pick up some writing tips, and then try them out in your own writing. Lots of top writers agree that using a notebook is a great way to capture ideas. Here are some websites where you can find interesting things to read:

www.childrenslaureate.org.uk

www.makewav.es

http://www.bbc.co.uk/writersroom/scripts   www.lovereading4kids.co.uk

www.carnegiegreenaway.org.uk/archive.php

READING 'THE WRITE WAY'

In this activity, pupils pair up to read a text together, before asking questions about the text to deepen their understanding and learning how to develop a discussion about the text.

Pupils will learn:

- ☑ to read, think and talk about a text.
- ☑ to ask higher-order question to deepen understanding.
- ☑ to listen and respond to the views of others.
- ☑ to speak confidently.
- ☑ how to analyse the choices good writers make.

Preparation:

1 Download or photocopy the Reading 'the write way' pupil page, enough for one between two, or display it on your interactive whiteboard.

2 Model some different ways to read a text together in a pair: one reads, the other listens; take turns to read a sentence or paragraph; both read aloud at the same time; take turns but stop at a tricky word to discuss its sound and meaning, etc.

3 Pupils will need some building blocks and a quality text.

Take it further!

- Select a pair to model their conversation to the whole class.

- Introduce different coloured blocks: one colour for agree statements and one colour for disagree statements, so the pupils can see how often they agree (or disagree!) with each other..

- Add a third role: a summariser, who listens to the conversation and takes notes, ready to feed back to the class.

- Assess the talk, or ask pupils to peer assess after devising their own criteria.

Mark's notes

There is solid evidence that paired reading is effective in developing reading confidence and fluency. The National Literacy Trust has an excellent toolkit called *Paired reading schemes: a teacher toolkit* to help you get started.

Pupils may find this type of activity difficult to start with, but it's worth persevering with because the better the reading questions, the better the writing is likely to be.

I have found that a short, time-framed writing task works well off the back of this activity. It can be as simple as 'write the next paragraph in the same style as the writer' or 'you've discussed what the writer is doing, now have a go yourself'.

You can find the Paired reading schemes toolkit here: **http://www.renlearn.co.uk/wp-content/uploads/2016/07/Paired-Reading-Schemes-a-teacher-toolkit.pdf.**

READING 'THE WRITE WAY' ACTIVITY

THINK about one of your heroes playing sport, acting, singing or dancing. Have you ever tried to copy them? In the same way, when you are reading, you can pick up tips from your favourite writers, but to do this you need to read as a writer.

Select a good extract from a text, and **READ** it with your partner.

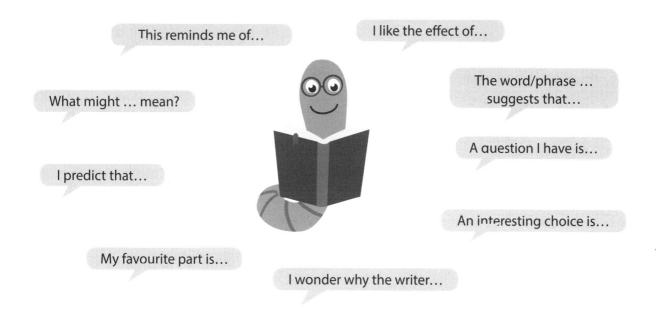

TALK to one another about the text, using the stems in the speech bubbles above to help you to read as a writer.

Once you've got the hang of the questions, find some building blocks. As you talk about the text, build a tower by adding a block every time you develop the discussion using any of the statements below:

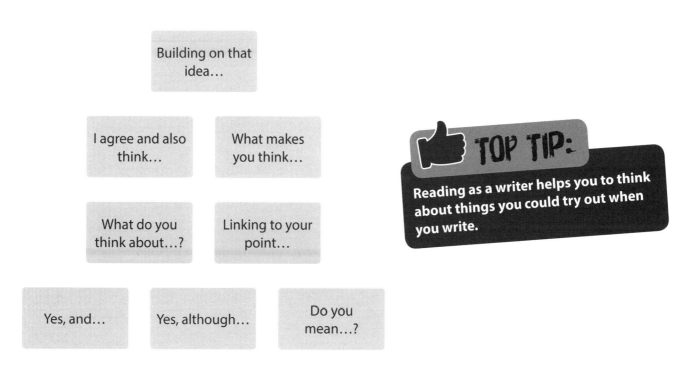

SENTENCE KNOCKOUT

In this activity, pupils consider what makes a good sentence, before evaluating sentences and justifying their opinions.

Pupils will learn:

☑ to evaluate the composition and effect of sentences.

☑ to read sentences closely with a critical eye.

☑ to express and justify an opinion.

☑ to collaborate and negotiate.

☑ how to find ideas and inspiration for writing by reading good writers.

Preparation:

1 Organise the pupils into pairs or groups.

2 Ask each group to draw a table like the one below on a large sheet of poster paper.

3 Make sure each group has at least 8 slips of paper and copies their selected sentences onto them.

Take it further!

• Organise a class 'Sentence of the week' competition, with the teacher adding to the draw as the week progresses.

• Set a ranking activity to focus on other writing features. Why not select other good texts and try the Sentence knockout activity with most dramatic verb; most effective noun or noun phrase; most colourful word or phrase; most emotive word or phrase; scariest sentence; or most vivid image?

Mark's notes

Perhaps it's the frustrated PE teacher in me which leads to most things turning into a game or competition – but trust me, this is a good one! It's a fun way to teach sentences but can get overly emotional for some pupils if they use their own sentences. It's safer to use sentences from their reading books, or at least make the sentences anonymous.

Quarter Final	Semi-final	Final	Winner

SENTENCE KNOCKOUT ACTIVITY

READ the two sentences in the shaded box below, from *The Wall* by William Sutcliffe. If the sentences were in a boxing match, which one would the judges make the winner? **TALK** to your partner and explain why you think that.

> In the corner are six old-looking fruit trees, planted in a perfect circle, forming what would once have been a shady grove.
>
> The trees are dead, with a scattering of dried-up leaves still clinging to the branches, but they surround a metal swing seat which looks as if it might work, as if it might be the only thing untouched by the carnage all around.

Extract © William Sutcliffe, 2014, *The Wall*, Bloomsbury Publishing Plc

THINK about how the judges would decide and the criteria they might use. **WRITE** a list of criteria for 'How to judge a good sentence'.

1 Working with a partner or a small group, write down eight good sentences on separate slips of paper – these could be your favourite sentences from your reading book; sentences written by your favourite writer; sentences written by your classmates; or the opening lines from your favourite books.

2 Place them face down, mix them up, then draw pairs of sentences to compete in the quarter-finals.

3 Now the fun part! For each pair of sentences, decide which sentence you think should go through to the semi-final and try to convince everyone else in your group. No bickering and no real boxing – you can vote to decide which sentence wins, or you could elect a judge to make the final decision. You could also score each sentence using the criteria you agreed on.

4 Place each winning sentence into the semi-final, ready to compete for a place in the final.

5 Repeat for the semi-final stage and then the final, after which you have a winning sentence to share with the rest of the class. Make sure you can explain how your group chose this sentence!

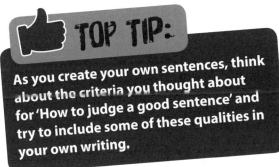

TOP TIP:

As you create your own sentences, think about the criteria you thought about for 'How to judge a good sentence' and try to include some of these qualities in your own writing.

TRAFFIC LIGHT QUESTIONS

In this activity, pupils ask and answer a progressive sequence of reading questions about a text.

Pupils will learn:

- ☑ to question the features and meaning of a text.
- ☑ how to explore the meanings of words through talk.
- ☑ to ask higher-order questions.
- ☑ how to find ideas and inspiration for writing by reading good writers.
- ☑ to work collaboratively with a partner.

Preparation:

1 Photocopy the pupil page, enough for one between two. The traffic light table would also work well as a laminated resource to support other questioning activities.

2 Project the first seven lines of the poem *Smile Please* by Roger Stevens onto the interactive whiteboard.

3 Organise pupils into pairs. I'd suggest pairing more-able readers with less-able readers.

4 Make sure pupils have access to rich texts – a selection of good poems around a theme would work well.

Take it further!

- Display a sequence of traffic light questions about a news story on the whiteboard at the start of the day.
- Change or add to the question stems.
- Apply the activity to a non-fiction text.

Mark's notes

You possibly ask up to 400 questions a day in your teaching role. The quality of these questions will determine the level of the thinking your pupils engage in, and it's an ideal opportunity to teach your pupils how to become skilled questioners themselves. This will have obvious immediate benefits to their learning but will also make them savvy in the longer-term, helping them 'get into the tester/examiner's head' when the dreaded tests and exams arrive.

Having looked at many SATs papers recently, it's clear that many pupils struggle to even attempt the higher-order questions – usually worth the most marks. This activity expects *every* pupil to attempt the higher-order question, but scaffolds their learning so that they progress to this question through the sequence. The more difficult 'green' question might be too daunting in itself, but the 'red' and 'yellow' questions prompt discussion about the context and the meaning, so that it becomes less daunting.

TRAFFIC LIGHT QUESTIONS ACTIVITY

THINK about the importance of writing as a reader and reading as a writer. Being able to ask a sequence of your own reading questions can really help you to do this.

READ the the first few lines of *Smile Please* by Roger Stevens and **TALK** to your partner about the best answers to the series of three traffic light questions below:

Red: When were the young men 'smiling for the cameras'?

Yellow: Can you explain why the young men were being photographed?

Green: Why do you think that the poet starts a poem about the Great War with images of smiling soldiers 'like they were going on holiday'?

Now, you are the questioner. Select another good text and **WRITE** your own sequence of three questions, choosing one from each column below. Then, swap questions with your partner and try to answer each other's reading questions.

Can you find a word similar in meaning to…?	Can you find evidence that…?	I wonder…
Which line/stanza/paragraph/sentence is about…?	Why do you think the writer has…?	What do you think about…?
What does …. mean?	True or false?	Why do you think…?
Who…?	How is this similar to…?	How effective is…?
What…?	What is different about…?	What might…mean?
Where…?	How does the writer…?	In your opinion, which is the best…?
Which…?	Can you predict…?	What would happen if…?
When…?	Can you explain…?	Why might the reader feel…?
Which of the following is correct? (multiple choice)	Do you agree that…?	What else does the writer…?

TOP TIP:

"Good learning starts with questions, not answers." Guy Claxton

ANNOTATION STATION

In this activity, pupils read and annotate a text to explore its themes, chains of words and patterns.

Pupils will learn:

- ☑ new vocabulary by listening to the responses of their peers.
- ☑ how to explore the meanings of words through talk.
- ☑ how to find ideas and inspiration for writing by reading good writers.
- ☑ how to identify and annotate the key features of a text.
- ☑ the effect of figurative language in a text.

Preparation:

1 Photocopy the annotated poems, or display these on your interactive whiteboard. If you are printing the poem – the bigger, the better.

2 Using the first poem, model how you would annotate a text and, if possible, share some good examples of annotated work.

3 Pupils will need highlighters (or coloured pencils) and rulers so they can have a go at annotating the second poem.

Take it further!

- Ask the children to perform the poem and think of an action to represent each line.

- Develop the idea further by using different texts to create a 'found poem'. You could show the pupils how to erase most of a text, leaving behind select words and phrases that make a poem; join together lines from different poems to form a new poem or; cut or tear up a text into words and phrases, then create a poem by rearranging them.

- Re-write the poem (or a line or stanza) in prose.

- Turn the poem into dialogue and act it out.

Mark's notes

Annotation is a skill which will continue to benefit pupils as they move up through the education system to the lofty heights of GCSE and A-level. The reading and talk are, of course, the most important elements, but I've always found that pupils are motivated by the artistic nature of this task.

Highlighting important words is just one way for them to annotate a text. Underlining or circling key words is also a good idea, and expecting pupils to make notes in the margin can help to generate rich talk about words and their effect, which is exemplary practice. Eavesdropping on this type of talk is a great assessment opportunity.

This process plants seeds for the writing to follow, as pupils consider how to make different choices to affect their reader in different ways. They will spot patterns – which add cohesion to a text – and this supports them to include patterns in their own writing.

We all understand how a limited vocabulary can be a real barrier for pupils, so best to start with a skim through and find words they might be unsure of, followed by some exploration of these words and their meanings.

A quick note on modelling:

Whilst modelling how to annotate a text using the first poem, explain that annotation is a way to notice and comment on features of a text. Underline or highlight Tennyson's notable choices, each in a different colour. You might include his choice of verbs; a pattern of prepositions; the rhyming pattern; the alliteration; his use of noun phrases; or a particularly powerful word. It's very important to model the language of possibility or uncertainty about a particular feature by using phrases such as 'I wonder why…' or 'It could be that…'.

ANNOTATION STATION ACTIVITY

THINK about how your teacher annotated the poem *The Eagle* by Alfred, Lord Tennyson. Highlighting words by underlining them or using coloured pens helps you to look at themes, chains of words and patterns in the text.

I have noticed a pattern of preposition phrases which show the reader the eagle's lofty position.

The Eagle

He clasps the crag <u>with</u> crooked hands;
<u>Close to</u> the sun in lonely lands,
Ring'd with the azure world, he stands.

The wrinkled sea beneath him crawls;
He watches <u>from</u> his mountain walls,
And like a <u>thunderbolt</u> he falls.

Alfred Lord Tennyson

I wonder why the poet has compared the eagle to a thunderbolt.

Where Go the Boats?

Dark brown is the river,
Golden is the sand.
It flows along for ever,
With trees on either hand.

Green leaves a-floating,
Castles of the foam,
Boats of mine a-boating—
Where will all come home?

On goes the river
And out past the mill,
Away down the valley,
Away down the hill.

Away down the river,
A hundred miles or more,
Other little children
Shall bring my boats ashore.

Robert Louis Stevenson

READ the poem *Where Go the Boats* by Robert Louis Stevenson. Around the poem, **WRITE** some notes about features you notice and why the poet might have chosen these features. **TALK** to your partner about the annotations you have made. What else do you notice? What do you think the poem is about? It could simply be about the poet's joy of launching 'boats' down the river, but could there be a deeper meaning?

TOP TIP:

When you write, think about your own word choices – can you develop a theme, chains of words and patterns for your reader?

READING RUMMY

In this activity, pupils develop confidence with the eight word classes which are underlined on the pupil activity page. They will also learn about some other grammatical features, which are given in bold.

Pupils will learn:

- ☑ how to scan a text for grammatical features.
- ☑ about aspects of grammar, e.g. phrases.
- ☑ to read, think and talk about words.
- ☑ to work collaboratively with a partner.

Preparation:

1 Photocopy the pupil page, enough for one between two, or display it on your interactive whiteboard.

2 Organise pupils into pairs.

3 Ideally, each pair needs its own pack of playing cards.

4 Revise any aspects of the tasks which pupils find difficult. Having a glossary on their tables works well, as does a classroom display.

Take it further!

- Rewrite the tasks and apply them to maths, Modern Foreign Languages or even places or features on a map.

Mark's notes

I first saw this idea being used by the excellent Year 6 team at Pevensey and Westham CofE Primary School. When I arrived in the classroom first thing in the morning, pupils were already playing a version of the game to practise their mental maths. This was a great way to ensure a purposeful and calm start to the day. Clearly, some of the pupils also liked adding a competitive edge to their game. I mentioned to the teachers that they could apply the idea to English and came up with this version later that day.

Once we venture away from the relative safety of a noun phrase, the world of phrases can be a confusing landscape. It will help pupils if you can model some examples to emphasise that a phrase serves the same function in the sentence as the head word does alone. You could use examples like:

The <u>man</u> walked towards us.

The <u>man from the shop on the corner</u> walked towards us.

The head word is 'man', and all the other underlined words make a phrase which acts like a noun. This is a noun phrase.

The girl was **tired**.

The girl was **as tired as she had ever been**.

The head word is 'tired', and all the other bold words make a phrase which acts like an adjective. This is an adjective phrase.

Preposition phrases are made from a preposition and a noun phrase, e.g. *under the cliff* or *before half time*. The phrase acts like a preposition.

READING RUMMY ACTIVITY

You will need a reading partner, an extract from a good text and a pack of playing cards.

TALK to your partner about what the bold and underlined words in the activity below mean, and look up any you are not sure of.

Look at your extract from a good text and **READ** the extract through individually. Then, take it in turns to select a card from the pack. The task for each card is shown below:

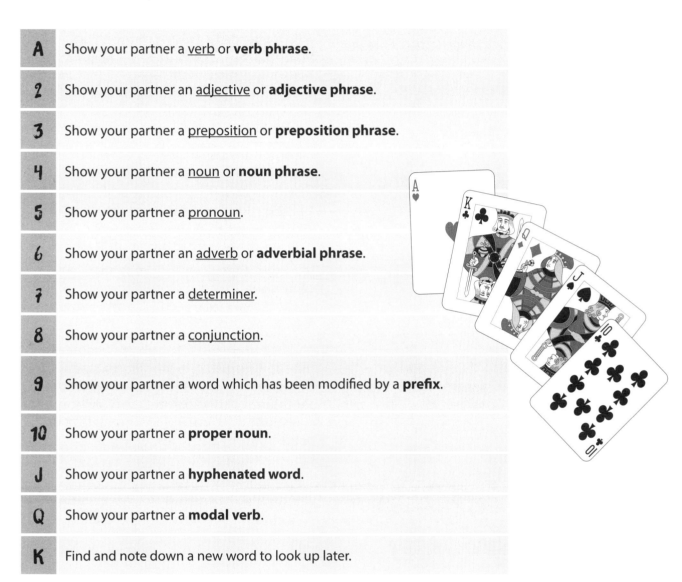

A	Show your partner a <u>verb</u> or **verb phrase**.
2	Show your partner an <u>adjective</u> or **adjective phrase**.
3	Show your partner a <u>preposition</u> or **preposition phrase**.
4	Show your partner a <u>noun</u> or **noun phrase**.
5	Show your partner a <u>pronoun</u>.
6	Show your partner an <u>adverb</u> or **adverbial phrase**.
7	Show your partner a <u>determiner</u>.
8	Show your partner a <u>conjunction</u>.
9	Show your partner a word which has been modified by a **prefix**.
10	Show your partner a **proper noun**.
J	Show your partner a **hyphenated word**.
Q	Show your partner a **modal verb**.
K	Find and note down a new word to look up later.

👍 **TOP TIP:**

Some of the cards ask you to look for phrases. When you write, think about how phrases can add detail and interest for your reader. A phrase is a group of words working together, which does not contain a subject and complete verb and is built around a head word. A phrase acts just like the head word would if it were on its own.

READING S.Q.U.A.D.

In this activity, pupils take on different reading roles to explore a text.

Pupils will learn:

- ☑ to stick to a particular role.
- ☑ to listen well.
- ☑ new vocabulary by listening to the responses of others.
- ☑ to apply a range of reading skills in a group setting.
- ☑ how to find ideas and inspiration for writing by reading good writers.

Preparation:

1 Photocopy the pupil roles, enough to slice and allocate to pupils, or display it on your interactive whiteboard.

2 Model a couple of examples to show pupils how you are thinking about the task and acting in the different roles.

Take it further!

- Make 'talk fans' with treasury tags for each role, for pupils to refer to as they contribute.
- Reduce the number of roles to start with if necessary.
- Give each pupil three coloured cards or sticky notes: A – green; B – blue; C – red. During a reading task, they are challenged to play each card – green when they *Agree* with and develop a point (A), blue when they *Begin* a new thread or idea (B) and red when they disagree or *Challenge* (C).

Mark's notes

When I attended a training course on oracy at the outstanding School 21 in Newham, I wrote down how a senior leader described talk in the school. She said, "Good talk is normal in every lesson and it's just part of good teaching."

Pupils will find this activity very difficult to start with – but expect them to persevere. Over time, they will master the skills through taking on the different roles in different tasks and you can raise the bar further by assessing their talk as evidence of their reading skills.

In a world where their thumbs do most of the communication, it's essential that we support pupils by making talk normal in our lessons, too.

My last tip is a practical one: these things take time, so allow plenty of time for groups to settle, learn and fulfil their roles. Commonly, the pressure of time results in the talk being squeezed out or rushed and we must fight this tendency.

READING S.Q.U.A.D. ACTIVITY

Reading a text together is an excellent way to share ideas. For this activity, you will need to be in a group of five or more. The members of your group will be in different reading roles to form a 'Reading S.Q.U.A.D'. Select a good text to **READ** and **TALK** about together. Organise your group into the five roles below – if you have more than five, then two people can share a role.

1. Starter and summariser	2. Questioner	3. Unpicker	4. Annotator	5. Devil's advocate*
Starts things off and might say:	Might ask:	Might:	Might:	Might say:
(During the discussion)	questions about the text	read key sections again	make notes about the text	I'd like to argue against that because…
I'm thinking that…	questions about what the others have said	read back and forth to find the meaning of something	underline key words and sections	Can you convince me that…?
The most important ideas are…	everyone if they are not sure about anything in the text	clarify (or ask the annotator to note down) things that are confusing	find patterns in the text and colour-codes examples, e.g. highlight adjectives which describe a character	That's true, but have you considered…?
The first thing we should talk about is…	'What do you mean by…?'	look things up in the dictionary or thesaurus		What about…?
To begin with, what do you think about…?	'Can you explain…?'		mark words which the group is not sure about	I disagree with you about…
(At the end of the discussion)'	'What do you think about…?'	research the answers to the group's questions		Have you thought about the opposite view…?
We all agree that…	'Who agrees with…?'	explain difficult words		
The main points were…	'What makes you think that?'			
A summary of the text is…				

*Devil's Advocate means someone who loves to argue, disagree or challenge. Hands up who just said 'No, it doesn't!'.

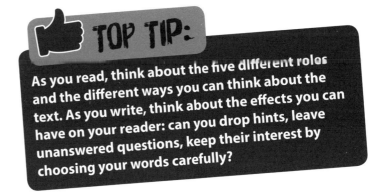

TOP TIP:

As you read, think about the five different roles and the different ways you can think about the text. As you write, think about the effects you can have on your reader: can you drop hints, leave unanswered questions, keep their interest by choosing your words carefully?

1

INVESTIGATE WRITING CHOICES TOGETHER

GRAMMAR BINGO

In this activity, pupils learn and revise key words from the grammar appendix of the National Curriculum in a fun way.

Pupils will learn:

☑ about aspects of grammar.

☑ to listen and talk well about grammar.

Preparation:

1 Photocopy the bingo card on the pupil page, enough for one each.

2 If you are very keen, or aspire to be on the stage, get some bingo balls for dramatic effect.

3 Organise pupils into pairs if they may need some support.

Take it further!

- Edit the groups of features to reflect the ability of a group.

- Delegate a feature to each pupil and ask them to write their own bingo call.

Mark's notes

Once the pupils have their cards and have chosen their words, you can call out the following bingo calls:

verb	A word in a sentence which tells the reader what is happening.
adverb	A word which tells the reader more about the verb.
pronoun	A word which can be used instead of a noun.
conjunction	A word which joins words, phrases and clauses together.
noun	A word which tells the reader the name of a person, place, thing or idea.
preposition	A word which shows the reader where or when something happens.
determiner	A word which modifies the meaning of a noun or noun phrase.
phrase	A group of words which work together.
clause	A group of words which includes a verb.
simple sentence	A sentence with one independent clause.
compound sentence	A sentence with two or more clauses joined by a co-ordinating conjunction.
adjective	A word which describes a noun.
complex sentence	A sentence with an independent clause and at least one dependent clause.
object (of a sentence)	What or who the subject of a sentence acts upon.
modal verb	A word like would, could, might, may, should.
subject (of a sentence)	What or who a sentence is about.
adverbial	A clause or phrase which tells the reader more about the verb.
preposition phrase	A group of words which shows the reader where or when something happens.
parenthesis	A word or phrase usually marked off by brackets, dashes, or commas.
subordinate clause	A group of words, including a verb, which does not make sense as an independent sentence.
relative clause	A clause which starts with 'who', 'which', 'where', 'when', 'whose' or 'that'.
noun phrase	A group of words which acts like a noun.

GRAMMAR BINGO ACTIVITY

THINK about the different types of grammatical features within your sentences. Good writers use grammar in a variety of ways, depending on the effect they want to have on their reader.

Select five grammatical features from group 1 and four from group 2. **WRITE** these into the blank spaces on your bingo card. Now, listen to the bingo clues and cross out any features which you hear described. If you cross out all your features, shout 'Bingo!'

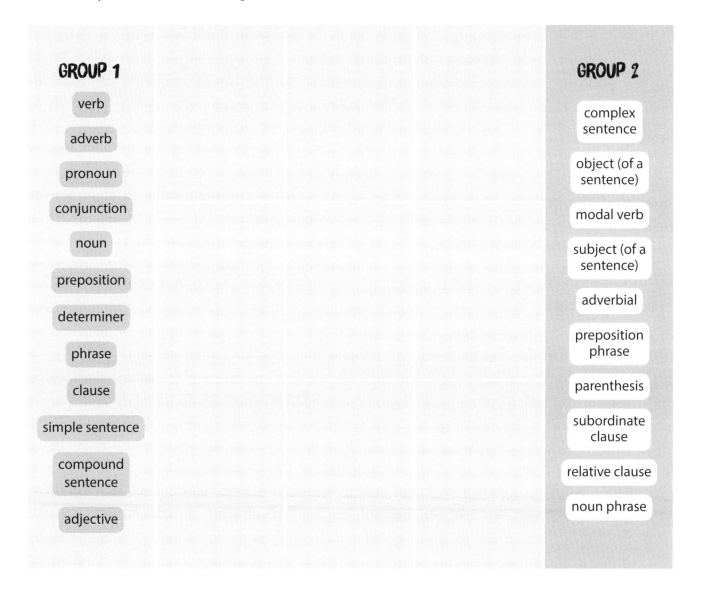

GROUP 1

verb

adverb

pronoun

conjunction

noun

preposition

determiner

phrase

clause

simple sentence

compound sentence

adjective

GROUP 2

complex sentence

object (of a sentence)

modal verb

subject (of a sentence)

adverbial

preposition phrase

parenthesis

subordinate clause

relative clause

noun phrase

TALK with your partner about your own writing. Which features from Grammar bingo would be easy to find in your writing? What might be more difficult to find?

READ a piece of your own extended writing. What patterns do you notice? What targets could you set yourself as a writer?

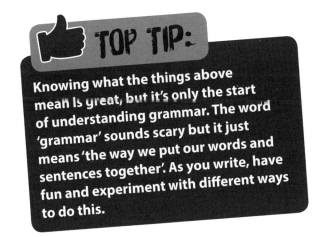

TOP TIP:

Knowing what the things above mean is great, but it's only the start of understanding grammar. The word 'grammar' sounds scary but it just means 'the way we put our words and sentences together'. As you write, have fun and experiment with different ways to do this.

Igniting Children's Writing © Mark McCaughan, 2018

DETERMINING DETERMINERS

In this activity, pupils think about what determiners are and how important they are in our sentences.

Pupils will learn:

☑ how to use determiners to modify the meaning of nouns and noun phrases.

☑ how to link different areas of learning.

☑ how to edit and change the meaning of a text.

Preparation:

1 Photocopy the pupil page, enough for one between two, or display it on your interactive whiteboard.

2 Model a couple of examples to show pupils how you are thinking about the task and using determiners.

Take it further!

• Have fun with the grammar and play 'Change the determiner, change the song title'. I'll start you off: One Hour from Tulsa; Either Girl is Mine; The Brick in Another Wall.

• Read the full version of the poem, and what becomes of the Jabberwock, at: **www.poetryfoundation.org/poems-and-poets/poems/detail/42916**.

• Print and laminate the pupil page to use as a word mat. This will act as a prompt to pupils as they apply their learning to start selecting determiners more independently.

• Teach pupils that phrases can also be used as determiners, e.g. <u>a few</u> people; <u>a couple</u> of people; <u>almost all</u> people.

Mark's notes

When the new National Curriculum was published, panic spread through the teaching profession like the waft of that 'little accident' in assembly. All of a sudden, seasoned, gnarly campaigners were confronted with terms they had not seen or uttered in 25 unblemished years of teaching. 'Determiner' was probably one of these terms.

I have heard determiners written off as 'those meaningless and unimportant words in a sentence' but this is untrue. For some pupils, being explicitly taught determiners can help them escape the rut that is 'the', 'a' or 'an' at the start of everything.

In the example on the pupil's page, when we change 'a battered life raft' to 'that battered life raft', or 'many battered life rafts', we are adding subtle layers of meaning – a valuable lesson for *all* pupils to learn.

DETERMINING DETERMINERS ACTIVITY

A determiner is always followed by a noun or noun phrase. It modifies the meaning of that noun or noun phrase.

READ the following sentence and talk to your partner about different words which could be used to replace the determiner 'a' in this example:

Far from shore, <u>a</u> battered life-raft drifted.

THINK about how changing the determiner can change the meaning of the sentence for the reader:

	Determiner	Noun phrase	
Far from shore,	a	battered life-raft	drifted.
Far from shore,	her	battered life-raft	drifted.
Far from shore,	that	battered life-raft	drifted.
Far from shore,	many	battered life-rafts	drifted.

READ the extract from *Jabberwocky* by Lewis Carroll in the centre of the table below. The words used as determiners are underlined for you.

a	some	several	other	no	most
an					more
the					many
this					either
that					neither
these					whose
those					few
my					every
your					enough
his					either
her					each
its					both
our	(any number)	their	all	another	any

(extract from) Jabberwocky by Lewis Carroll, 1832–1898

'Twas brillig, and <u>the</u> slithy toves
Did gyre and gimble in <u>the</u> wabe:
All mimsy were <u>the</u> borogoves,
And <u>the</u> mome raths outgrabe.

"Beware the Jabberwock, <u>my</u> son!
<u>The</u> jaws that bite, <u>the</u> claws that catch!
Beware <u>the</u> Jubjub bird, and shun
<u>The</u> frumious Bandersnatch!"
He took <u>his</u> vorpal sword in hand;
Long time <u>the</u> manxome foe he sought—
So rested he by <u>the</u> Tumtum tree
And stood awhile in thought.

And, as in uffish thought he stood,
<u>The</u> Jabberwock, with eyes of flame,
Came whiffling through <u>the</u> tulgey wood,
And burbled as it came!

Around the extract, there are words which can be used as determiners. **WRITE** the poem on a separate piece of paper, but replace each determiner with another from the table to see how you could change the meaning and sound of the poem.

TOP TIP:
Try adding a wider range of determiners to your nouns when you write.

CONJUNCTION FUNCTION

In this activity, pupils think about conjunctions, how they are used and the different meanings they can create.

Pupils will learn:

- ☑ how to read for aspects of grammar.
- ☑ how to use conjunctions and additional clauses to develop sentences.
- ☑ how to write compound and complex sentences.

Preparation:

1 Photocopy the pupil page, enough for one between two, or display it on your interactive whiteboard.

2 Model a couple of examples to show pupils how you are thinking about the task and how conjunctions can be used to join words, phrases and clauses.

3 Pupils will need a coloured pen or pencil.

Take it further!

- Have a conjunctions display, word mat or washing line in your classroom so that pupils become familiar with the words, can use them during talk tasks and can select from a wider range. As a minimum, display: *than, because, while, where, after, so, though, although, since, until, whether, before, once, nor, like, yet, unless, for, whereas, whenever.*

- Add 'conjunction' to a sentence starter display. ISPACED (a display which suggests ways to start a sentence) has its limitations but has an immediate impact on sentence variety so is worth a go for a couple of weeks. **ISPACED** can stand for:
  I – an -ing verb ending;
  S – a simile;
  P – a preposition;
  A – an adjective;
  C – a conjunction;
  E – an -ed verb ending;
  D – dialogue.

Mark's notes

This activity focuses on how conjunctions can be used for effect. I have become weary of moderation meetings where I hear, 'There's a "because" so that's his complex sentence.' The first thing we should be asking is, 'Is the sentence any good?' Then, 'Does that sentence work well in this piece? Would it be better if it wasn't a complex sentence but a sentence fragment or a simple sentence?' Later, we might say, 'This writer has a good range and variety of sentences, and some of them happen to be complex, so there's plenty of evidence for that descriptor.'

Conjunctions are one of the many connectives that writers can use, including conjunctive adverbs, adverbial phrases and clauses, and reference chains. Conjunctions are single words. All conjunctions are connectives, but not all connectives are conjunctions, and that's what this activity teaches.

CONJUNCTION FUNCTION ACTIVITY

THiNK about when we use words as conjunctions. These are single words which are placed at the junction between words, phrases and clauses. Imagine them as junctions on a train line.

READ the two sentences below and **TALK** to your partner about how joining them with different conjunctions affects the meaning of sentence:

Patrick was happy. Manchester United had beaten Chelsea.

Patrick was happy and Manchester United had beaten Chelsea.

Patrick was happy although Manchester United had beaten Chelsea.

Patrick was happy whenever Manchester United had beaten Chelsea.

Once Manchester United had beaten Chelsea, Patrick was happy.

In a Year 6 class I know rather well, pupils are awarded a raffle ticket for excellent work. On the back of this raffle ticket, they write down an activity for their 'perfect day' at the end of term. At the end of term, there is a raffle and the activities which are picked make up their perfect day. **READ** 'My perfect day' below and draw a station under all the conjunctions. Think about how the conjunctions are used, the effect they have and where they have been placed in the sentences.

My perfect day by Lottie, aged 11

Seriously though, we could meet at forest school, make our own fire and cook a campfire breakfast after making mud sculptures. Before returning to school, we could have a treasure hunt and a game of 'capture the flag'. Back at school, it would be movie club (with popcorn) because we'd need a rest. Next we could organise a class bake off although we are still clearing up from last time. That would leave enough time for a Lego building competition and a sports tournament before home time. Perfect!

WRiTE your own 'perfect day'. As you write, choose your conjunctions carefully and think about where to place them to create interesting sentences. You could even try to persuade your teacher that the perfect day raffle is a good idea for the end of term!

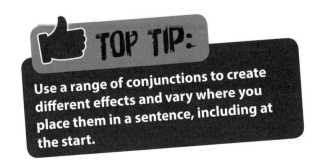

TOP TIP:

Use a range of conjunctions to create different effects and vary where you place them in a sentence, including at the start.

PASSIVE PIZZA

In this activity, pupils get to ponder and practise the passive voice.

Pupils will learn:

- ☑ how to use the passive form of verbs.
- ☑ how to vary their sentences for effect.
- ☑ how to think about their reader's needs.

Preparation:

1 Photocopy the pupil page and display it on your interactive whiteboard.

2 Using the passive pizza, model how you would construct a passive sentence or clause, e.g. Beaten for the first time this season… (clause). Chelsea were beaten for the first time this season (sentence).

Take it further!

- Ask the pupils to underline the passive voice in a text. Photocopy the short story, <u>Disgruntled</u>, below.

Mark's notes

Sometimes it's difficult to find evidence of the passive voice in a pupil's writing. However, it's not that hard to find if you read a range of texts, such as newspapers (Mrs. Smith sacked by Jones), non-fiction texts (Polar bears are threatened by receding ice), recipes (After the soufflé has been burnt, phone a takeaway), etc. So, if passive constructions are too hard to find, this may indicate that the pupil's reading diet hasn't been broad enough.

This activity will help to teach the passive voice and then this can be added to the pupils' writing toolkit. Once you've taught this, and displayed the icon, expect pupils to apply it occasionally, choosing when it works best. You can download more writing toolkit icons at **www.mcmlearning.co.uk**.

"Enter, Timothy," Mrs. Kidney-Pie the headteacher bellowed from her office, or Interrogation Cell 1 as the pupils referred to it. "Now, Timothy, four window panes have been smashed, a prize tomato plant has been squashed and we have a very disgruntled caretaker. Would you mind recounting your activities at playtime?"

Timothy knew that the very future of football in the playground depended on his answer. "I'm awfully sorry, Mrs. Kidney-Pie," began Timothy, whose face was turning a shade of red to rival the new Man Utd home kit, "It seems probable that, having considered all the possibilities, the ball was kicked over the fence and the greenhouse may, or may not have been, that is to say, smashed, hence the disgruntled nature of the caretaker. By the way, may I, on behalf of all the pupils, extend our very best wishes to Mr. Overall – and we sincerely hope that he is feeling gruntled again soon."

Igniting Children's Writing © Mark McCaughan, 2018

PASSIVE PIZZA ACTIVITY

TALK to your partner about the meaning of subject, verb and object. Most sentences are active, in that the subject performs the verb and the object receives the verb, e.g. The lion (subject) eats (verb) the springbok (object).

If we put the springbok first, it is still receiving the verb but becomes the subject of **a passive sentence**, e.g. The springbok is eaten by the lion. Passive sentences often have a preposition after the past participle. These are the 'extra toppings' on our passive pizza.

With a partner, work your way around the passive pizza below to **WRITE** a passive sentence:

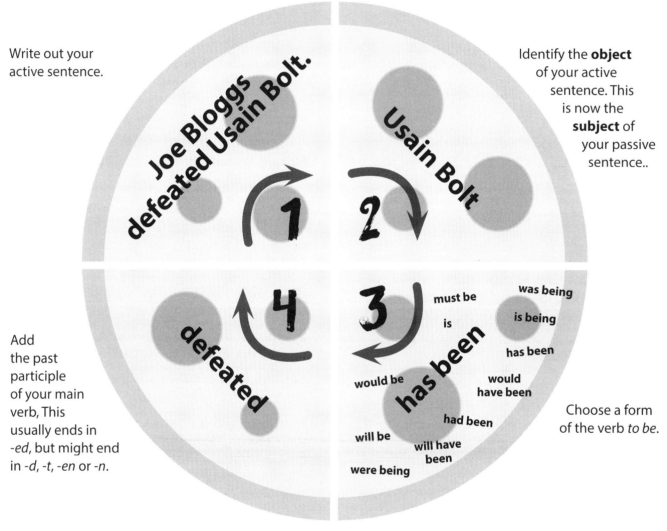

Write out your active sentence.

Identify the **object** of your active sentence. This is now the **subject** of your passive sentence..

Add the past participle of your main verb, This usually ends in -ed, but might end in -d, -t, -en or -n.

Choose a form of the verb *to be*.

Joe Bloggs defeated Usain Bolt.

Usain Bolt

defeated

has been

must be
is
was being
is being
has been
would be
would have been
had been
will be
will have been
were being

TOP TIP:

Think about how you could use passive sentences in your writing. Writers often use the passive form of verbs when the object is more interesting than the subject (Usain Bolt has been defeated by Joe Bloggs); to hide the subject (Anya was being followed); or to make the reader sympathise with a character (Graham was bullied).

5 If you want to, add another topping:

by Joe Bloggs

in a dramatic 100m race

at the Olympic Stadium

CERTAINLY, PROBABLY AND POSSIBLY MODALS

In this activity, pupils think about modal verbs and how these can help to express certainty, probability and possibility.

Pupils will learn:

☑ about aspects of grammar.

☑ how to use different forms of verbs.

☑ how to discuss an issue, considering different points of view.

☑ that modal verbs can be used as a persuasive device.

Preparation:

1 Photocopy the pupil page, enough for one between two, or display it on your interactive whiteboard.

2 Download some resources from ROSPA (**www.rospa.com/leisure-safety/water/advice/ tombstoning**) to support the pair talk and provide a reading opportunity.

Take it further!

- Add a modal verb toolkit icon to a display once this has been taught, with the expectation that pupils use this skill when an opportunity arises.

- Display the table of modal verbs for a short period.

- Replace tombstoning with a local issue – there could be a good assembly there!

Mark's notes

It shouldn't be the case, but the modal verb can be another feature which is hard to find in a pupil's range of writing evidence. This is avoidable if we look for writing opportunities from across the curriculum. How about:

Plenary in maths How else could you solve that problem?

Geography How much rainfall do you predict the weather station has recorded overnight?

RE/PSHE Faced with that situation, what could you do? What should you do?

History Why might Boudicca want to resist the Roman invasion?

Science List three possibilities: what could happen when we add the water?

Beat the teacher Make three sporting predictions for this weekend.

From a purely English point of view, there should be no shortage of opportunities to read, model and write modal verbs through dilemmas faced by characters; dialogue; any tasks which look into the future; and when considering why a writer might have made a particular choice.

If we set high-quality tasks which lend themselves to considering certainty, probability and possibility, we'll certainly start seeing modal verbs.

CERTAINLY, PROBABLY AND POSSIBLY MODALS ACTIVITY

THiNK about the picture and text below, which are from website of the Royal Society for the Prevention of Accidents (ROSPA):

Tombstoning – 'Don't jump into the unknown'

Tombstoning is an activity which has occurred around the coast for generations. Unfortunately, over recent years it has gained attention for the wrong reasons, with a number of people (typically male teenagers) killed or seriously injured. The title was adopted because of the way a person falls and plunges into deep water, in a similar way a stone would.

Why is it dangerous?

- Tombstoning offers a high-risk, high-impact experience but it can have severe and life-threatening consequences. This is because:

  - Water depths alter with the tide – the water may be shallower than it seems

  - Submerged objects like rocks may not be visible – these can cause serious impact injuries

  - The shock of cold water can make it difficult to swim

  - Getting out of the water is often more difficult than people realise

  - Strong currents can rapidly sweep people away

TOP TIP: As you write, think about using modal verbs to express certainty, probability and possibility.

Imagine you are with a sports team on tour. The tournament is at a seaside resort. This evening, the activity is a trip to the pier. You are in a group of six and people start daring one another to jump off the pier into the sea. Other groups are doing it and it looks fun. Eventually, your best friend is accused of being a 'chicken' and agrees to be the first one to leap.

TALK with your partner about how you both feel about the situation above. One type of verb which can help is a *modal verb*. Speak in complete sentences, and try to use some modal verbs shown below in your sentences. As you use each modal verb, put a tick by it.

☐ can	☐ can't
☐ could	☐ couldn't
☐ may	☐ may not
☐ might	☐ might not
☐ ought to	☐ ought not to
☐ shall	☐ shan't
☐ should	☐ shouldn't
☐ will	☐ won't
☐ would	☐ wouldn't

WRiTE no more than 150 words, in which you must persuade your best friend to stay safe. Use modal verbs to help you.

GRAMMATICAL SENTENCES GAME

In this activity, pupils explore the effects of different grammar choices in their sentences.

Pupils will learn:

☑ aspects of grammar, e.g. adverbials, clauses, conjunctions.

☑ to consider their own grammar choices as they approach independent writing.

☑ to talk and share ideas about grammar.

☑ to select and reject different writing choices.

Preparation:

1 Photocopy the pupil page, enough for one per group or pair, or display it on your interactive whiteboard. This works well as a laminated mat for repeat use.

2 Model an example to show pupils how you are thinking about the task and making changes to a simple sentence. Choose a theme from the learning journey for the pupils to write their first sentence about.

3 Pupils will need two dice and a counter.

Take it further!

- Return to this activity to teach that not all sentences are structured subject–verb–object. You could challenge pupils to come up with a subject–verb sentence (Faye laughed), an object–verb–subject sentence (Adam was chased by the cow), or an object–verb sentence (Arsenal were defeated again).

Mark's notes

At this stage in the sequence, investigating grammar together supports pupils of all abilities, in a non-threatening way, to feel confident about grammar. Later in the sequence, they will face their own choices, and the draft sentences they are working on here might be useful at this stage.

Set one important ground rule: Stop working on a sentence as soon as further changes start making it sound silly. A longer sentence is not necessarily a better sentence. In fact, during the editing phase of the sequence, it will be important to teach pupils to take out superfluous words. Once they are happy with a sentence, they should start working on another.

Regular, practical, collaborative grammar opportunities like this are bound to ensure that pupils are confident and well prepared for the KS2 test.

GRAMMATICAL SENTENCES GAME ACTIVITY

READ the instructions for the game below and **TALK** to your partner about what the grammatical terms mean, e.g. clause, adverbial. Before you start the activity, **THINK** together about the words you're not sure of and check these on the working wall, in your dictionary or ask your teacher.

WRITE your simple sentence and get started. You will need two dice and a counter.

THE RULES

Roll the dice and move around the board, modifying your sentence each time you land on a square. Stop whenever you are happy with your sentence.

What happens when you add or change a determiner? **1**

Re-read your sentence – does it sound right? Is it punctuated correctly? **16**

What happens when you turn the sentence around? **15**

What happens when you take something away? **14**

Can you change the meaning by changing one word? **13**

What happens when you add an adverbial before the verb? **2**

Can you make a phrase from a noun, verb, adjective, adverb or preposition? **12**

What happens when you add an adverbial after the verb? **3**

Can you change the meaning by changing one word? **11**

What's the effect of making a noun phrase? **4**

What happens when you expand a noun phrase? **10**

What happens when you add a conjunction and a clause? **5**

What's the effect of placing an adverbial at the start of the sentence (a fronted adverbial)? **6**

What's the effect of embedding a relative clause starting with *who*, *whose*, *whom*, *which*, *where*, *when*, or *that*? **7**

What happens when you add a conjunction and a clause? **8**

What's the effect of embedding a relative clause starting with *who*, *whose*, *whom*, *which*, *where*, *when*, or *that*? **9**

👍 **TOP TIP:**

There is no right or wrong where sentences are concerned – grammar is just a word that means 'how we choose to put our sentences together in different ways'. As a writer, experiment with different choices and then choose the sentence you like best, or that works best for your reader.

TIME TRAVELLER

In this activity, pupils think about how to move their reader backwards or forwards in time, or how to keep them in the moment.

Pupils will learn:

☑ that verbs take on a different form for different tenses.

☑ how to use modal verbs to help other verbs.

☑ to consider their own grammar choices as they approach independent writing.

☑ to talk and share ideas about grammar.

Preparation:

1 Photocopy the pupil page, enough for one between two, or display it on your interactive whiteboard.

2 Model an example to show pupils how you are thinking about the task and using prepositions.

3 Pupils will need two different-coloured highlighters or pencils, two dice and two counters.

Take it further!

- Adjust the writing task so the pupils can write about a hobby, a sports team, a famous person, a character from a book or your learning journey topic. As they write, the pupils guide the reader through the past, present and future of the topic.

- Have pupils take up different roles, including a note-taker, who records the different verb forms. These notes can then be used to support the writing task.

Mark's notes

Tenses are often taught in a very inflexible way. (Reminder: bin those grammar worksheets, especially that one about the subjunctive mood in past-progressive, passive sentences!) This activity plants the seeds of a flexible and explorative approach to tenses, because, in reality, we use tenses flexibly and we jump around, even in the same sentence. For example, we might say, 'Yesterday, I was thinking about how I will be at Maud's wedding this time next week, and now I'm in a panic about what on Earth I'm going to wear.' I think it's more important for pupils to have their audience in mind, and to check through their writing for clarity, than to be bogged down in the feeling that a piece of writing must stay in the same tense – because it's not true. (As for Maud's wedding, I went for a little black slip dress with a fascinator from the pound shop.)

You could model this to the pupils, with something related to their learning journey, like: 'In the early 20th century, Ernest Shackleton made several unsuccessful attempts to reach the South Pole but he is still admired today as a skilled explorer and leader.'

TIME TRAVELLER ACTIVITY

THINK about how you can take your reader forward and backward in time. To do this, writers add suffixes like -ed, -en and -ing to verbs, as well as using helping verbs.

READ the text below. In one colour, highlight where suffixes are used to change the endings of verbs. In another colour, highlight where the writer has used any of the helping verbs.

> Generating electricity from wind power is an alternative to burning fossil fuels; it produces no greenhouse gas emissions during operation, consumes no water, and uses little land. This is not a new idea, though. People have used the power of the wind for thousands of years, using it to power machines which pumped water onto fields or ground grain to make flour. With global climate change becoming more of a concern, it is likely that wind power will continue to rise in popularity, so look out for wind farms which may dominate your local landscape in years to come.

The best way to practise using helping and modal verbs is to **TALK** your sentences through with a partner, and the time traveller game will help you to do this:

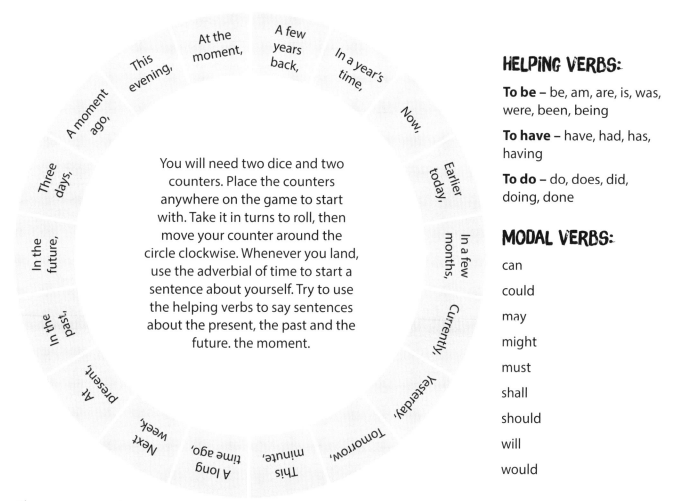

You will need two dice and two counters. Place the counters anywhere on the game to start with. Take it in turns to roll, then move your counter around the circle clockwise. Whenever you land, use the adverbial of time to start a sentence about yourself. Try to use the helping verbs to say sentences about the present, the past and the future. the moment.

This evening, / At the moment, / A few years back, / In a year's time, / Now, / Earlier today, / In a few months, / Currently, / Yesterday, / Tomorrow, / This minute, / A long time ago, / Next week, / At present, / In the past, / In the future, / Three days, / A moment ago,

HELPING VERBS:

To be – be, am, are, is, was, were, been, being

To have – have, had, has, having

To do – do, does, did, doing, done

MODAL VERBS:

can

could

may

might

must

shall

should

will

would

Choose a moment from a film, a book or a picture. **WRITE** about this moment, then take the reader backwards and forwards in time from the moment.

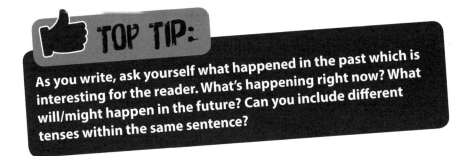

TOP TIP:

As you write, ask yourself what happened in the past which is interesting for the reader. What's happening right now? What will/might happen in the future? Can you include different tenses within the same sentence?

TIME FOR THE ADVERBIALS OF TIME

In this activity, pupils think about using adverbials to organise shifts in time in their writing.

Pupils will learn:

☑ to vary the structure of their sentences.

☑ to engage the reader with additional information in adverbials.

☑ to consider their own grammar choices as they approach independent writing.

☑ to talk and share ideas about grammar.

Preparation:

1 Photocopy the pupil page, enough for one between two.

2 Find an image from the book *When Jessie Came Across the Sea* by Amy Hest and display it on the interactive whiteboard.

3 Use the tables on the pupil page to model some examples to show pupils how you are thinking about adding adverbials as you add them to different parts of a sentence.

4 Getting the pupils to draw their own blank tables might be a useful scaffold for some.

Take it further!

- Encourage pupils to find their own interesting picture to write about, and use the Time for the adverbials of time pupil page to structure their writing.

- Swap the image for one which relates to your class text or learning journey.

- Use the same idea for adverbials of place or manner.

Mark's notes

A teacher I was working with once had a major breakthrough with her class through a minor action: she put the words 'how', 'where' and 'when' above the whiteboard. As soon as pupils were encouraged to think of these prompts, there was an immediate impact on the writing, especially as the emphasis was on showing your reader how, where and when.

This activity encourages pupils to rehearse the tense of each sentence by including an adverbial of time, which may be omitted in the final written version.

Like with all aspects of grammar, you could raise the expectations of pupils by including a skills-based learning intention such as 'We are learning to using adverbials of time to guide our reader', and this can then become your assessment focus.

Over time, it's good practice for pupils to be encouraged to free themselves from the shackles of teacher-prescribed learning intentions, but they will need these if learning something for the first time.

TIME FOR THE ADVERBIALS OF TIME

READ the extract below, from the wonderful book *When Jessie Came Across the Sea* by Amy Hest, which tells the story of a young girl's journey from Eastern Europe to a new life in America. **READ** the image your teacher has displayed on the board. **TALK** to your partner about how the characters might be feeling and how you can tell.

On a fine fall day, they sailed past the Statue of Liberty. America! No one swapped stories or argued. Babies hushed. Even the oldest passengers, and the most seasick, stood against the rail. America!

Although we've already learnt that we don't always need to stay in the same tense, it's easy to confuse your reader if you write in the wrong tense at the wrong time. A good way to avoid this is to say, and then write, an adverbial of time at the start of every line. This will keep your sentence in the tense you want it to be in. In the examples below, the writer is writing as Jessie.

adverbial of time	the rest of the sentence
Right now,	I am gazing in awe at the New York skyline.
Right now,	the ship has fallen silent as hundreds of us huddle excitedly on the deck.
Right now,	I wonder what my future holds.
Right now,	there is no looking back.

In the same way, you could take the reader back in time, as Jessie looks back:

adverbial of time	the rest of the sentence
A few weeks ago,	my heart was breaking when the rabbi told me I had to leave the village.
A few weeks ago,	I had looked back at Grandma, who waved from the dock as the ship pulled out to sea.

The sentences can be developed them by replacing or removing the time adverbials:

adverbial of time	the rest of the sentence
With the Atlantic wind stinging my face,	I am gazing in awe at the New York skyline.
	The ship has fallen silent as hundreds of us huddle excitedly on the deck.
At the start of our long voyage,	I had looked back at Grandma, who waved from the dock as the ship pulled out to sea.
Now,	there is no looking back.

Now, **WRITE** your own sentences and develop them by replacing or removing the time adverbials.

TOP TIP:

Don't forget to separate your adverbials with a comma, and use your adverbials to add interesting detail for the reader.

SENTENCE FACTORY

In this activity, pupils think about the structure of sentences and the different choices writers make.

Pupils will learn:

- ☑ how to think about their reader's needs.
- ☑ to consider their own grammar choices as they approach independent writing.
- ☑ to talk and share ideas about grammar.
- ☑ to select and reject different writing choices.

Preparation:

1 Photocopy the pupil page, enough for one between two, or display it on your interactive whiteboard.

2 Model an example to show pupils how you are thinking about the task and how to progress through the sequence of activities.

3 Pupils will need a dice and some letter tiles.

Take it further!

- Create a smartboard version of the activity, with the letters chosen randomly and the software's dice feature.
- Incorporate a dictionary activity as the pupils select the words for their initial sentence.

Mark's notes

Like the other activities in this section, this can be shared as a whole-class activity, a starter, a paired task or a group task. The more silliness, the better, so encourage pupils to be creative with their initial sentence, e.g. H J K could be 'Hippos juggle their knickers.'

The dice consequences require pupils to identify, understand and use several grammatical features which they'll be tested on in SATs week. Much more importantly, it teaches them to apply these features their writing with confidence once they are familiar with them.

You could develop this by teaching that sentences don't have to have an object. Ask your pupils to write sentences which are made up of:

a. subject + verb

b. object + verb + subject

c. object + verb.

They could choose one of these to put through the sentence factory.

SENTENCE FACTORY ACTIVITY

All sentences have a *verb* (the doing, being or having word in the sentence), and a *subject* (the person, place, thing, or idea that is doing, being or having). Some sentences also have an *object* (these words *receive* the action). **READ** the examples below:

Subject	Verb	Object	
The naughty boys	threw	stones.	
Messi	scored	the winning goal.	
A blue whale	eats	krill.	
Despite its immense size,	a blue whale	eats	krill,	a minute crustacean.

Read the last sentence again carefully. **TALK** to your partner about how you could change the other sentences by adding words before, after or in-between the subject, verb and object.

THINK about all the interesting ways we can play around with our sentences. You will need some letter tiles, a dice and this pupil page. Here's how to play:

1 Pick three letters and write a basic subject–verb–object sentence using the letters you have chosen, for example, H J K could be '**H**enry **j**ousted with a **k**night'.

2 Roll the dice and follow the instructions in the first column to build on your sentence.

3 Lastly, roll the dice a second time and follow the instructions in the second column to complete your sentence.

1	Make the subject a pronoun.
2	Put the object first to make a passive sentence.
3	Add a relative clause (starting with who, whose, which, where, when or that).
4	Add an adverbial of time, manner or place.
5	Add a conjunction and a clause to the start of the sentence.
6	Make a noun phrase.

1	Expand a noun phrase.
2	Make the object a pronoun.
3	Change a word or phrase.
4	Change the sentence type (statement, question, command or exclamation).
5	Add a conjunction and a clause to the end of the sentence.
6	Make the subject a pronoun.

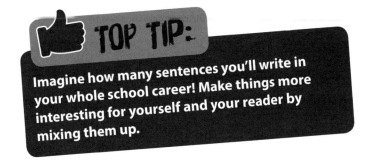

TOP TIP:
Imagine how many sentences you'll write in your whole school career! Make things more interesting for yourself and your reader by mixing them up.

Igniting Children's Writing © Mark McCaughan, 2018

THE AMAZING MODIFIER MACHINE

In this activity, pupils learn about the subtleties which can be achieved by modifying words with adverbs or adjectives.

Pupils will learn:

☑ to select and reject different writing choices.

☑ to explore and make phrases.

☑ to read, think and talk about words.

☑ how to think about their reader's needs.

☑ to infer subtle differences made by different writing choices.

Preparation:

1 Photocopy the pupil page, enough for one between two. This works well as a laminated mat.

2 Model an example to show pupils how you are thinking about the task and using modifiers.

Take it further!

- Use other suggested words in the same activity, e.g. cold, calm, frightening, happy, dark, heavy, dangerous, curious, quiet, good, slow, young, wet, hot, stormy, sad, anxious, light, excited, worried, noisy, evil, fast, old, rough, or dry.

- Develop this into a further reading task, e.g. Can you find modifiers in your reading book? What happens when you change the modifier? What effect do you think the writer was trying to create?

Mark's notes

When you read Greater Depth Standard writing, you may not even notice the choices the pupils have made because you are too engrossed to worry about the grammar. All the features are there, but they are used seamlessly and precisely. Often, what sets these pupils apart from their peers is the subtlety in their writing.

This is a useful activity for teaching how to achieve this subtlety. It's also an opportunity to bring the reading and the writing close together, a key strategy if we want our pupils to read as writers (and vice versa). Through the initial reading task, pupils infer shades of meaning – good preparation for when they write.

THE AMAZING MODIFIER MACHINE ACTIVITY

THINK about how we can make the meaning of our words more specific by adding words which are used as adjectives or adverbs – these are called *modifiers*. **READ** the sentences below and **TALK** to your partner about how the effect of the sentence changes as the word 'calm' is modified by the added words. Note that modifiers can come before or after the word being modified.

The sea is **calm.**

The sea is **really calm.**

The sea is **never calm.**

The sea is **almost calm.**

The sea is **not calm.**

The sea is **calm for now.**

Plot the modifiers above on the line below. More intense modifiers go on the left; less intense modifiers go on the right. Can you think of any other ways 'calm' could be modified? **WRITE** your ideas on the Amazing Modifier Machine, selecting the best place to position them.

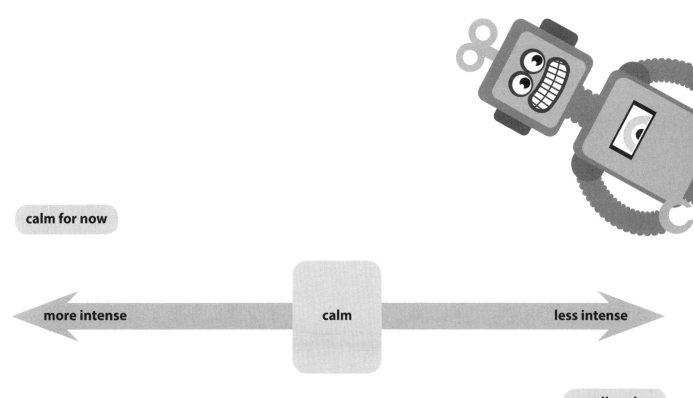

calm for now

more intense ← calm → less intense

really calm

Choose another word to place in the machine. How many different ways can you modify its meaning?

Now, select your most effective phrase and include this in the opening line of a piece of writing. As you write, think about the effect you can create by modifying words and phrases.

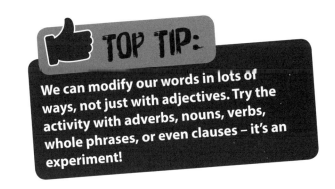

TOP TIP:

We can modify our words in lots of ways, not just with adjectives. Try the activity with adverbs, nouns, verbs, whole phrases, or even clauses – it's an experiment!

CRICKET CLAUSES

In this activity, pupils learn about and practise independent, dependent and relative clauses.

Pupils will learn:

- ☑ how to vary the structure of their sentences for effect.
- ☑ how to read for independent and dependent clauses.
- ☑ to consider their own grammar choices as they approach independent writing.
- ☑ to talk and share ideas about grammar.
- ☑ key vocabulary in context.
- ☑ how to explore the meanings of words through talk.

Preparation:

1 Prepare a list of key words, phrases or themes from your class reading book, your learning journey or a unit of work in a particular subject. The pupils will each need two coloured pencils.

2 Photocopy the pupil page, enough for one per group, or display it on your interactive whiteboard with your own key words.

3 Model a couple of examples to show pupils how you are thinking about the task and using clauses in different ways to speak about the list of key words.

Take it further!

- Introduce the reporting clause into the scoring system.

- Use this as a start-of-day activity, with key words from yesterday's learning, or key words from news stories of the week.

- Introduce key words at the start of a topic, e.g. 'We are going to learn about the school grounds as a habitat for wildlife. Can you predict what our key words are going to be?'

- Include key quotes from a play or a poem.

- Use some of the words for spelling activities and ask pupils to add tricky words to their personal spelling list.

Mark's notes

This is a very simple idea, under the guise of a game of cricket, but it's excellent for reviewing learning, building subject knowledge, generating rich talk and creating links between different areas of learning. As such, it's a good example of how English grammar should be taught – to facilitate deep thinking and learning. If pupils practise this type of joined-up thinking and talking, they will have a chance to write in a joined-up way. After all, if they can't say it, how will they write it?

CRICKET CLAUSES ACTIVITY

THINK about how words can form *clauses*. A *clause* is a group of words which has a *verb* and a *subject* for the verb. If a clause makes sense on its own, it is called an *independent clause* and could be used as a sentence. Clauses which do not make complete sense on their own are called *dependent clauses*.

READ the following sentences and **TALK** to your partner about the clauses in the sentences. Then, underline independent clauses in red and dependent clauses in blue:

The fox crossed the field, sniffing for food.

Sniffing for food, the fox crossed the field.

The fox, which was sniffing for food, crossed the field.

> Hint – the independent clause may be separated into different parts!

A dependent clause which starts with a relative pronoun (*who* or *whose*, *which*, *where*, *when* or *that* is called a *relative* clause). These are good for adding detail and making links in your sentences.

Let's practise relative clauses by playing Cricket clauses. Here is a cricket pitch with some key words from the Year 5 science curriculum.

THE RULES

1 Take it in turns. When it is your turn, your opponent 'bowls' to you by choosing a word from the cricket pitch.

2 Build clauses to make a sentence about the word.

3 Set a time limit and keep the score. Game on!

SCORING

1 run for a one-clause sentence about your word.

2 runs for a two-clause sentence about your word.

4 runs for a sentence which includes a relative clause starting with who, whose, which, where, when or that.

6 runs for a sentence which includes a relative clause starting with who, whose, which, where, when or that, *and* which contains another word from the game board.

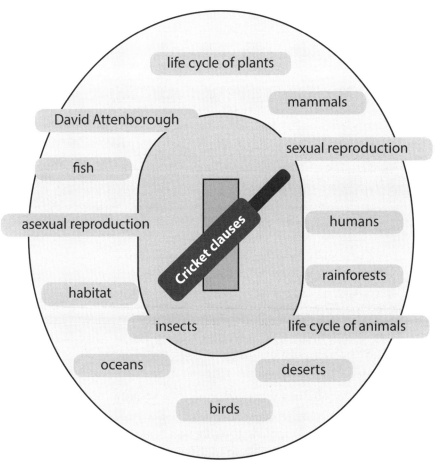

WRITE a paragraph of no more than 100 words about something from your current learning journey. Use clauses in different ways and try to link your ideas together.

TOP TIP:

The example above features content from the Year 5 science curriculum but you can add your own words to the game – these could be key words from a chapter of your reading book, key words from a topic or a group of words linked to any theme.

ALIEN NOUN PHRASER

In this activity, pupils think about the questions which will enable them to write engaging noun phrases.

Pupils will learn:

- ☑ how to develop a head noun into a noun phrase.
- ☑ to consider the details which will engage and interest the reader.
- ☑ to consider their own grammar choices as they approach independent writing.
- ☑ to talk and share ideas about grammar.
- ☑ to ask questions which improve their writing.

Preparation:

1 Photocopy the pupil page, enough for one between two. This works well as a laminated mat.

2 Display the first stanza of the poem *Timothy Winters* by Charles Causley on the interactive whiteboard.

3 Model an example to show pupils how you are thinking about the task and asking questions to develop your noun phrases.

Take it further!

- Use the activity to improve writing in different subjects. For example, 'easily-eroded, sedimentary chalk' on a diagram in science or geography might work better than simply 'chalk'.

- Play 'What's in the box?' with pupils using the noun phraser questions to deduce what you are hiding.

- Play 'What or who am I?' by putting a sticky note with the name of an object or person on a pupil's back. They then mingle in the room and guess their identity using the noun phraser questions.

Mark's notes

This is an old favourite of mine. I have used versions of this idea with pupils in KS1 all the way up to ~~horrible~~ hormonal and hard-to-settle GCSE groups. It always works a treat, and I usually turn the questions into a fan of cards joined with a treasury tag, for pupils to use as a scaffold for their conversation.

We need to be wary that being over-descriptive for the sake of it, or showing off how well they can use the thesaurus, can be a limiting factor for some pupils. So, it's important to add the caveat that they must keep control and make sure that the noun phrases add to the piece, particularly in certain genres. A noun phrase like: 'The accused, who is 25 and lives in Brighton' might work well in a news report but 'The man in the dock, who shops at Asda and was wearing an "I'm With Stupid" t-shirt' would not.

ALIEN NOUN PHRASER ACTIVITY

THiNK about noun phrases, and how these can help writers to describe nouns in more detail for the reader.
READ the stanza from the poem that is projected on the whiteboard and identify any words which are used as nouns. **TALK** to your partner about which of the nouns are part of a group of words which acts together as a noun in the sentence. I'll get you started: 'school' is a noun on its own, whereas 'Timothy Winters' is a group of words which act together as a noun – this is called a *noun phrase*. How many others can you find in the first stanza of the poem?

ALiEN NOUN PHRASER QUESTiONS:

How old?

Moves like?

Feels like?

Sounds like?

Looks like?

Made of?

What colour?

How big?

Tastes like?

Look at a piece of your partner's writing or perhaps an object in the room you're in, and choose a noun (on its own). Imagine that you are describing this noun to an alien from the Planet Fidgetus Spinnittus V. (Luckily, they speak English there.)

Working together with your partner, how many noun phrases can you build from your chosen noun by firing the questions in the Alien Noun Phraser at it? **WRITE** them here as you come up with them, then each of you should choose your best one and add it to your writing.

....

....

....

....

....

👍 **TOP TIP:**

Another thing to remember about noun phrases is that they are made from any group of words which can be replaced by a pronoun. For example, 'The tall girl with the yellow hoodie and blue trainers, the ones that I've always wanted, who is sitting over there and who is eating an apple and listening to Little Mix told me', could be replaced by 'She told me'.

STARTER MENU

In this activity, pupils think about their choice of sentence starters and use the starter menu to consider the range of choices they can use themselves.

Pupils will learn:

- ☑ to vary the structure of their sentences.
- ☑ to apply aspects of grammar, e.g. word class.
- ☑ to consider their own grammar choices as they approach independent writing.
- ☑ to talk and share ideas about grammar.
- ☑ to select and reject different writing choices.

Preparation:

1 Photocopy the pupil page, enough for one between two, or display it on your interactive whiteboard. This works well as a laminated mat for repeated use.

2 Model a couple of examples to show pupils how you are thinking about the task and using different starters from the menu, and the effect these have.

3 If the full starter menu is overwhelming, display the activity on the board and reduce the choices or conceal some of the squares. Perhaps you could conceal them all to start with and ask the class to predict what's on there.

Take it further!

- Prepare pupils with a reading task – how many different ways to start a sentence can you find in your own writing? How many ways can you find in something by your partner or your favourite writer?

- Write a five-sentence 'backwards story'. Start by writing the last sentence at the bottom of the page, then working up towards the start. Use a

Mark's notes

If you've ever tried writing, you'll know that getting started can be the hardest skill of all. Before writing that sentence, for example, I made a cup of tea, rummaged through the cupboards to find the crisps my wife hides from me and emptied the dishwasher, as shameless avoidance tactics – because I felt stuck.

This activity models the myriad of starter choices we have and should help pupils to avoid this 'stuck' feeling. Previously I mentioned the ISPACED display (I3) as a simple strategy to accelerate progress. The ideal we are working towards is that, over time, pupils are not reliant on scaffolds, displays or word mats. That said, it is undeniable that they are useful as they learn a skill. After all, if they are starting sentences with conjunctions, they are constructing more complex sentence structures – something you can highlight in your assessment.

STARTER MENU ACTIVITY

READ the text below. What do you notice about the start of each sentence?

> The new Ferrari Formula One car is certainly setting tongues wagging in the paddock. The distinctive red car with the prancing horse shield is more streamlined this year, with an arrow-like chassis and improved cooling system. The improvements helped Ferrari driver Sebastian Vettel record the fastest time of today's testing. The best lap of 1m 19.024s, set on Pirelli's ultra-soft tyres, was three-tenths of a second quicker than the second-placed Mercedes of Lewis Hamilton. The Ferrari team will be feeling confident about the season ahead as the opening race of the season in Melbourne approaches.

Sometimes, simple words like 'I', 'The' or 'A' can be the most effective choice at the start of your sentences. However, if your sentences usually start the same way, it could get pretty boring for your reader. So, select a couple of sentences from the text above and change the way they start by choosing from the 'Starter menu' below. I can't believe prawn cocktail isn't on there! (I dare you to try and start a sentence with it, though.)

Starter menu				
A conjunction: And But So Although While After As Before Once Since Until When While Like Though Whereas Because If Unless	a word ending in 'ly'	a colour	a noun phrase	an adverb/adverbial of time (when)
	a word ending in 'ed'	a number	a preposition/ prepositional phrase	an adverb/adverbial of place (where)
	a word ending in 'ing'	an adjective	a name	an adverb/adverbial of manner (how)
	a word ending in 'en'	a simile	a pronoun	a proper noun
	alliteration	onomatopoeia	a modal verb (can, could, may, might, would, should, won't, shall, will etc.)	a verb
	a list of three	something spoken	a food	personification
	a touch	a taste	a question	a smell
	a noun	a feeling	a sound	a sight
	words which rhyme	a determiner	an exclamation (e.g. What!)	a determiner

TALK with your partner and create a story, taking it in turns to say the next sentence and starting each sentence with a different choice from the menu above.

WRITE your story using the best bits of the talk, starting each sentence in a completely different way.

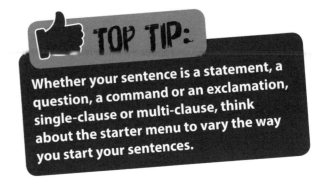

TOP TIP:

Whether your sentence is a statement, a question, a command or an exclamation, single-clause or multi-clause, think about the starter menu to vary the way you start your sentences.

Igniting Children's Writing © Mark McCaughan, 2018

T

TRY OUT
INDIVIDUAL CHOICES

PRE-LAUNCH CHECKLIST

In this activity, pupils start to plan their own piece and ask themselves questions about what they hope to achieve in their writing.

Pupils will learn:

- ☑ how to start making independent writing choices.
- ☑ how to consider the audience, purpose and genre of their writing.
- ☑ how to think creatively about bringing their writing to life for the reader.

Preparation:

1 Photocopy the pupil page, enough for one each. This works well as a laminated A3 mat for repeat use.

2 Model an example to show pupils how you are thinking about the task and exploring possibilities, discounting some ideas and perusing others.

3 Adapt the pre-launch checklist based on the needs of your pupils. There is a simpler version in the downloads area of **www.mcmlearning.co.uk**.

Take it further!

- Build up the menu of choices as the year progresses after starting with a simpler version.

Mark's notes

The full checklist is aspirational and something to aim towards, especially for those pupils aiming for Greater Depth standard. I know – there's a lot in it! I'd suggest identifying some key areas which fit well with the particular writing task you're teaching. I'd also suggest that this doesn't drag on – keep it timed and snappy.

Although we need to be careful not to overwhelm the pupils, this is a really important activity and stage of the writing process. This is when the seeds of independent writing are planted: we've worked on lots of words, reading tasks, explored grammar together – now it will be your own choices which count.

Pitching the task in this way will reduce the chance of every pupil having largely the same piece of writing to meet over-prescriptive learning intentions. From the outset, pupils are encouraged to think about how they can put their own stamp on the piece.

The in-flight entertainment section was inspired by some of the best writing I've seen in my years as a moderator: a main piece, complemented by an embedded collection of supplementary pieces. These can be a brilliant opportunity to show shifts in formality, so it's worth challenging pupils to build them into their planning.

PRE-LAUNCH CHECKLIST ACTIVITY

You are now on the launchpad of your writing task, about to create the best piece of writing you have ever produced. Before you take off, it's a good idea to plan your flight! **TALK** to your partner and **THINK** about the choices which will work best in your piece of writing.

What's the purpose? (e.g. to inform, to persuade, to recount, to entertain, to argue, to explain, etc.)

Who's the audience? (Who are you writing for?)

What's the best genre? (What are you going to write, e.g. letter, story, play script, leaflet, etc.?)

What's the key content?		What are the key ideas?		Who are the key character(s)?
Main point of view (circle)	**First person** (I, me, we, mine, my, us, our, ours)	**Second person** (you, your, yours)		**Third person** (he, she, it, him, her, his, hers, its)
Main tense (circle)	**Past tense** (looking back)	**Present tense** (in the moment)		**Present tense + helping verbs** (looking into the future)

Level of formality (make a mark on the continuum)

very informal ⟷ very formal

Prose?	Poetry?	**Text organisation** (tick)
Fiction?	Non-fiction?	☐ heading and sub-headings
		☐ one paragraph
Based on my reading, the **grammar choices** I'm going to try out are:		☐ many paragraphs
1.		☐ a list with commas/semi-colons
		☐ a list with bullet points
		☐ columns
2.		☐ stanzas
		☐ free verse
3.		☐ diagram

In-flight entertainment (circle)

Ideas for a good beginning	Ideas for a good ending	a picture and caption	a text message
		a ticket	a bill
		a menu	a sketch
		a ration card	a travel plan
		a picture collage	a diary entry
		a tweet	a secret code
What do I need to research	Key words and phrases	a postcard	a text box
		a labelled map	a cartoon
		a quiz	a thought bubble

READ through your planning notes and then start to **WRITE**. 5...4...3...2...1...Lift off!

PREPARE TO PLAN

In this activity, pupils think about different ways to make a simple plan before setting out their own piece of writing.

Pupils will learn:

☑ how to structure texts in different ways.

☑ to consider the needs of their reader.

☑ about thinking maps.

☑ how to link different areas of learning.

Preparation:

1 Photocopy the pupil page, enough for one between two, or display it on your interactive whiteboard. Each of the templates is available as a separate download from www.mcmlearning.com.

2 Model a couple of examples to show pupils how you are thinking about the task and using the planning templates.

Take it further!

- Assess the planning as a skill in itself.

- Provide some of the plan for those pupils who may need support whenever they are writing a piece.

- Use sticky notes so that pupils can move ideas around and try out different options.

Mark's notes

Different types of text need different types of plan. Arguably, free-writing doesn't need a plan but most texts would certainly benefit from one. If pupils learn to draft out the stanzas of a poem, the text boxes of a leaflet, the progressive paragraphs of a persuasive text, etc., then their finished text is more likely to be organised and coherent.

It's also amazing how much impact a simple plan can have on the balance of a finished piece. Often, writing is at its best in the first few lines and then tails off. This activity puts equal weighting to all areas of the text, and sometimes it works well to encourage pupils to plan the end or the middle first.

The plans also generate excellent thinking and the links and connections created by this thinking should transfer to the writing, making it more cohesive and coherent.

PREPARE TO PLAN ACTIVITY

THiNK about the planning shapes below and **TALK** to your partner about which shape might work best for: comparing different things or ideas; structuring a story; building an argument; organising a persuasive text; setting out an information text; organising events into order; creating a poem. Can you think of any other planning shapes that might be useful?

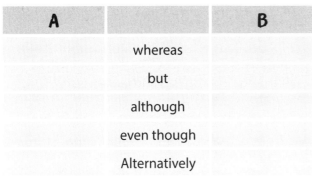

A		B
	whereas	
	but	
	although	
	even though	
	Alternatively	

Might work well for planning:

....

Might work well for planning:

....

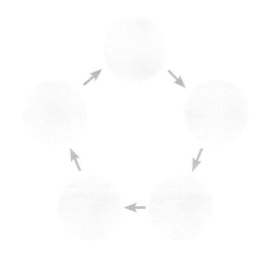

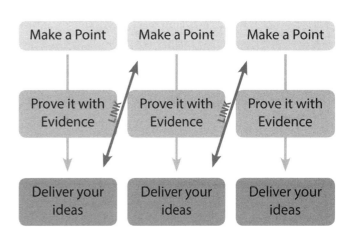

Might work well for planning:

....

Might work well for planning:

....

Choose a planning shape and **WRiTE** a plan of your own about: the dos and don'ts of school discos; How to make the perfect camp; Why whaling should be banned; The tastiest-ever take away; Pele or Messi: who's best?; My favourite day; or The similarities and differences between my three favourite books.

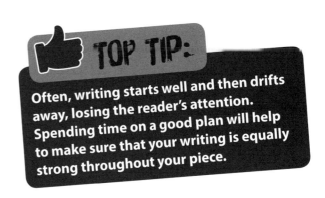

TOP TIP:

Often, writing starts well and then drifts away, losing the reader's attention. Spending time on a good plan will help to make sure that your writing is equally strong throughout your piece.

PARAGRAPH POWER-UP

In this activity, pupils think about when a new paragraph is needed and how to build a quality paragraph.

Pupils will learn:

- ☑ how to structure texts in different ways.
- ☑ to consider the needs of their reader as they draft their paragraphs.
- ☑ how to link different areas of learning.
- ☑ to use paragraphs accurately.

Preparation:

1 Photocopy the pupil page, enough for one each, or display it on your interactive whiteboard.

2 Model a couple of examples to show pupils how you are thinking about the task and asking questions to help you build a paragraph.

Take it further!

- Create a display with your top tips for paragraphs. Use icons as well as words to make the learning stick. Something like:

  - Start a new paragraph when you change **time**.

  - Start a new paragraph when you change **place**.

  - Start a new paragraph when you change **topic**.

  - Start a new paragraph when you change **person or character** (including every time the speaker changes in dialogue).

Mark's notes

I am very surprised that 'The pupil can write for a range of purposes and audiences using paragraphs to organise ideas' is a KS2 descriptor for Working Towards the Expected Standard, because I have always found that most pupils struggle to paragraph well. They may be leaving a gap, but is the gap in the right place, and is the paragraph itself well put together and serving a clear purpose? This drafting activity uses a model to show pupils this 'putting together' process and the type of writing questions which can help them.

PARAGRAPH POWER-UP ACTIVITY

THINK about when you should start a new paragraph in your writing. **TALK** to your partner about how to complete this sentence:

Start a new paragraph when you change **t**..........., when you change **p**.............., when you change **t**.............. or when you change **p**................. or character (including every time the speaker changes during dialogue).

When you start each new paragraph, it's important to 'power-up' the paragraphs, so that they keep your reader interested. **READ** through the plan below (for a paragraph about where a particular breed of dragon lives) and think about how you could 'power-up' your own paragraphs.

1 Write a topic sentence to signal what the paragraph is about.
This species of dragon lives in unexpected places.

....

2 What could you include to grab the reader's attention?
It is normally found in the lofts of normal houses, in normal streets, in normal towns just like yours.

....

3 Which nouns or noun phrases might work well?
these shady corners
a warm place to sleep

....

4 Which verbs or verb phrases might work well?
lurking
patiently waiting
breathing fire

....

5 Which prepositions or preposition phrases might work well?
above you
through gaps in the tiles
under the cover of darkness

....

WRITE your own paragraph plan above before writing a powered-up paragraph of your own in your book. Start with a topic sentence (it doesn't have to be about dragons!) and then follow the steps to create a tip top paragraph.

 **TOP TIP:**

Try to make links between your paragraphs. A good way to do this is to mention something from the paragraph before. For example, the topic sentence of my next paragraph in the dragon piece could be, 'Now you know that the dragons might live just above your head, would you like to know what they eat?'.

REFERENCE CHAINS

In this activity, pupils think about adding a sense of cohesion to their writing by including reference chains.

Pupils will learn:

☑ how to avoid disengaging repetition.

☑ how to construct noun phrases to inform and engage the reader.

☑ how to read for patterns in a text.

☑ how to think about their reader's needs.

☑ how to draft ideas to include in their writing.

Preparation:

1 Photocopy the pupil page, enough for one between two, or display it on your interactive whiteboard.

2 Model an example to show pupils how you are thinking about the task and highlighting a reference chain – why not use the first text box with the repetition of 'basking shark'?

Take it further!

• Ask pupils to read older pieces of writing to look for the presence (or absence) of reference chains.

• Scaffold a piece with gaps for pupils to fill.

• Read for reference chains in other texts: sports reports, travel articles, biographies, etc.

Mark's notes

Having worked on words, read as a writer and investigated choices together, this stage of the sequence is about pupils drafting their ideas and trying out different choices. They do this supported by the foundation of the learning earlier in the sequence.

This activity teaches one aspect of drafting – in this case, chains of reference which will make the end-piece more cohesive. If pupils don't consider the cohesion in the whole text prior to writing, it will be difficult for them to add this at the editing stage.

Regarding the top tip, this makes an important point to the pupils. The reference chain is not just to avoid repetition, but can be an effective and concise way to include meaningful information for the reader, which strengthens the complete text.

REFERENCE CHAINS ACTIVITY

What do you **THINK** about this homework entitled 'My favourite animal'? **TALK** to your partner about how it could be improved.

My favourite animal is the Basking Shark. Basking Sharks have been around for 11 million years. Basking Sharks can grow to 11 metres in length and Basking Sharks can weigh up to seven tonnes. The Basking Shark's jaws can reach 1 metre wide because Basking Sharks filter large amounts of water. The Basking Shark is the second largest fish in the world although the Basking Shark is the biggest fish in British waters.

What's that you say? Oh, very well, I've re-written it without being quite so repetitive. **READ** the version below and highlight any words or phrases which replace the phrase 'the Basking Shark'. Then, join the words together from top to bottom as a chain. This chain, connecting all the shark references, is called a **reference chain**.

My favourite animal is Britain's largest fish and the second largest fish in the world. The Basking Shark has graced our oceans for millions of years. It can grow to 11 metres in length which is approximately the size of a London bus. This friendly giant weighs up to seven tonnes — that is roughly equivalent to six cars. Its cavernous jaws can reach 1 metre wide because it filters large amounts of water to feed on microscopic organisms called plankton. They are often mistaken for Great White Sharks although bashful Basking Sharks are completely harmless to humans.

Equally impressive to its size is the Basking Shark's adaptability to different habitats. Found worldwide, the much-travelled species prefers cooler waters but can also survive in the much-warmer waters at the equator. It can often be spotted close to land whenever it swims at the surface. Spotters should make the most of their encounter before this adaptable creature plunges down to its maximum depth of 910 metres.

Sadly, despite its adaptability this magnificent creature is not safe from humans. The Basking Shark is vulnerable because it is curious and will approach boats. This, and the fact that it is a slow swimmer, makes the shark easy to catch. It is caught for its skin, which is used as leather; its fin, which is used for soup and its cartilage, which is used in traditional Chinese medicine. The population of this species is declining rapidly and if we continue to kill the Basking Shark in such numbers it will soon be extinct. Let's hope these endangered sharks are to grace the oceans for another million years - perhaps humans will have to adapt their behaviour!

WRITE your own reference chain. How many different ways can you think of to name… a sports star; a musician; a hobby; a pet; or a place?

Now, **THINK** about how you could write about your chosen topic and include words and phrases from your reference chain.

TOP TIP: Reference chains are also a good way to add information for the reader. Think about what the reader learns from 'these endangered sharks' or 'bashful Basking Sharks'.

PERUSE BEFORE YOU CHOOSE

In this activity, pupils play a dice game to practise the skill of trying out different writing choices before evaluating each choice to select the best one.

Pupils will learn:

- ☑ how to select and reject different writing choices.
- ☑ how to explore different ways to structure their sentences.
- ☑ aspects of grammar, e.g. clauses, phrases.
- ☑ that punctuation can be used for effect.
- ☑ how to think about their reader's needs.

Preparation:

1 Photocopy the pupil page, enough for one each, or display it on your interactive whiteboard.

2 Model some examples to show pupils how you are thinking about the task and responding to different dice rolls.

3 Pupils will need a dice each.

Take it further!

- Use this as a whole-class starter activity.
- Edit the dice consequences to match the needs of your class, or the needs of a particular task.
- Ask pupils to make their own dice table, based on their personal writing targets, e.g. 1 = Check a spelling. 2 = Change a conjunction, etc.

Mark's notes

Of all the activities in the book, I think this one is the single most effective and I'd recommend using it often. It models to pupils that writing evolves from messy beginnings to a polished end-product, and this end-product will emerge from hundreds of small decisions and changes. Just like a masterpiece has its origins in the sketch book, the quality texts you have been reading earlier in the sequence were inevitably crafted in this way, so this could be explained and modelled to the pupils.

Perfect presentation is for the end of the sequence only and we mustn't let presentation get in the way of creativity and experimentation. When you are assessing the writing, this activity produces the best evidence possible because it gives an insight into the writer's choices and broadens the range of skills they have demonstrated. Often, the best evidence lies in the 'scruffy stuff'.

Regarding the top tip, this is where the W.R.I.T.E.R. sequences works well when you have planned some breaks in the lesson sequence, allowing pupils to return to their work with fresh eyes. They may have written something on Tuesday, and on Thursday your starter could be for them to re-read the work and highlight any weaker areas. Then, try out some different possibilities.

PERUSE BEFORE YOU CHOOSE ACTIVITY

THINK about how changing words, phrases, punctuation marks or the order of your words can change the meaning of a sentence. When John Lennon scribbled the words for *Lucy in the Sky with Diamonds* on a tatty sheet of paper, he wrote 'Look for the girl with the sun in your eyes – and she's gone'. Later, he crossed out the word 'your' and replaced it with 'her'. How did changing this word change the meaning of the line? Like an artist sketching out different ideas, good writers try out different possibilities and then select the best possibility for the effect they want.

WRITE your own simple sentence below the example.

Example sentence:	Snowdrops fell to the ground.
Your sentence:	

Now, roll a dice and rewrite your sentence based on the number you roll:

Try out possibilities for a single word and select the best one.

Example: ~~Snowdrops~~/~~Snowflakes~~/<u>A flurry of snow</u> fell to the ground.

Your sentence:

Try out possibilities for building or changing a phrase.

Example: Snowdrops fell to ~~the ground~~/<u>the waiting ground</u>/~~the fields below~~.

Your sentence:

Try out possibilities for adding a clause.

Example: Snowdrops, <u>which swirled in flurries</u>, fell to the ground. ~~and swirled before settling~~.

Your sentence:

Try out possibilities for changing the order of your sentence.

Example: ~~Snowdrops fell to the ground~~/<u>The frozen ground was gradually covered by the falling snow</u>.

Your sentence:

Try out possibilities for changing the effect by changing the punctuation.

Example: ~~Snowdrops, swirling, swooping, fell to the ground.~~/<u>Snowdrops fell; they blanketed the ground.</u>

Your sentence:

Try out possibilities for shortening or lengthening your sentence.

Example: ~~Snow fell.~~/<u>Snowdrops fell</u>, ~~covering the town~~/<u>until the town was snug in a white blanket</u>.

Your sentence:

TALK with your partner about the writerly choices each of you has made. Which choices are the most effective? What advice would each of you give the other?

READ through other pieces of your writing. Can you find any sentences you could improve using the Peruse before you choose game?

WRITE a piece which includes your original sentence. As you write, think of suitable places to 'peruse before you choose'.

SENTENCE PALETTE

In this activity, pupils think about the four types of sentence and consider how these can be combined when they write.

Pupils will learn:

- ☑ how to structure texts in different ways.
- ☑ how to scan for and annotate grammatical features.
- ☑ how to write negative sentences.
- ☑ to talk and share ideas about grammar.

Preparation:

1 Photocopy the pupil page, enough for one between two, or display it on your interactive whiteboard.

2 Collect some children's newspapers to use as a stimulus for the second part of the activity. Alternatively, you could use a photo from your current topic.

3 Model a couple of examples to show pupils how you are thinking about the task and using different sentences in different ways. The negative sentence would be a powerful type to model, e.g. if I've written: 'The leading rider takes off the ramp', what would happen if I changed that to: 'The leading rider doesn't miss the chance to accelerate over the ramp'?

Take it further!

- Display a space-related picture if you want to pursue the Tim Peake theme. Tim Peake's excellent resources can be found online at **www.stem.org.uk/esero/resources**.

- Use the Sentence palette as a display or a laminated mat.

Mark's notes

This activity could work nicely in a sequence with the Starter menu (I13) so that pupils make the connection between how they start a sentence and the type of sentence they are writing. You could pose some questions like: is it only questions you can make when you start with a question word? Which types of sentence can you make when you start with a verb? Can all four types of sentence be both positive and negative?

At this stage of the sequence, when we are supporting pupils to 'get on and write', it's important not to stall and get bogged down in grammar. So, this activity needn't take long, but it holds an important question for the pupils to think about as they write – which works best here?

SENTENCE PALETTE ACTIVITY

THINK about the four types of sentence: statement, question, command and exclamation. **READ** the paragraph below and see if you can annotate each type of sentence:

Look above you, out into space, and imagine orbiting the Earth at an altitude of 205 miles. That's what Tim Peake experienced for the first time, as he arrived at the International Space Station in 2015. The British astronaut spent six months on board the ISS, where he carried out educational projects designed to attract young people into science, and inspire the next generation of space travellers. Was the project successful? Only time will tell, but look around you: which of your classmates could be the next Tim Peake, or perhaps give the Martians a fright as one of the first Earthling settlers on Mars? It could be you. What a thought!

When you write, think of the different types of sentence you can choose to make your writing interesting. You could think of this set of choices as an artist's palette:

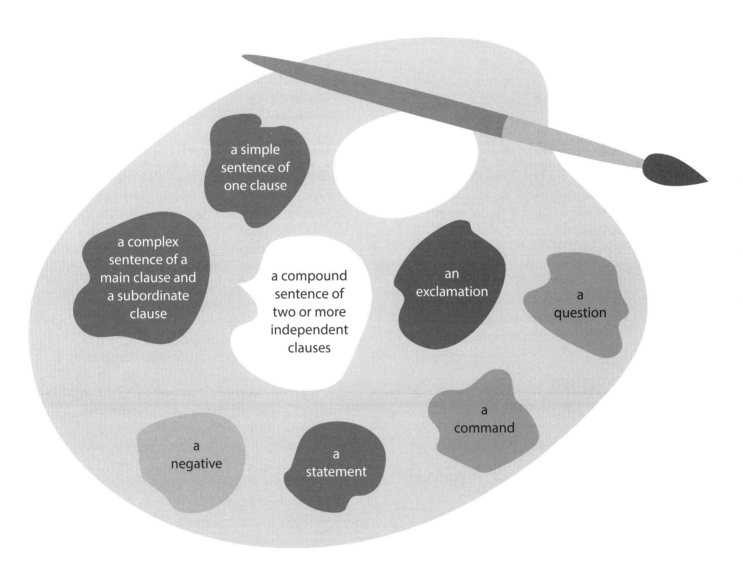

Choose a picture from the newspaper with your partner. **TALK** with them about the picture.

WRITE some sentences inspired by the picture, trying out different sentence types from your sentence palette.

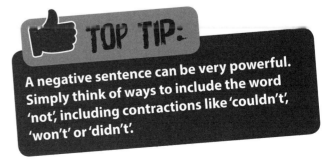

TOP TIP:

A negative sentence can be very powerful. Simply think of ways to include the word 'not', including contractions like 'couldn't', 'won't' or 'didn't'.

CHARACTER BUILDING

In this activity, pupils think about bringing their characters to life for their reader by observing and describing fine details.

Pupils will learn:

- ☑ to be observant and create a sense of the real world in their writing.
- ☑ how to think about their reader's needs.
- ☑ how to think creatively about bringing their writing to life for the reader.
- ☑ to select and reject different writing choices.
- ☑ how to write descriptively.

Preparation:

1 Photocopy the pupil page, enough for one per group, or display it on your interactive whiteboard.

2 Model an example to show pupils how you are thinking about the task and using the questions on the pupil page.

Take it further!

- Ask pupils to create their own table following a talk activity. How about: what are the fine details we can observe when we are 'people watching'?

- Play a 'Who am I?' game – pupils describe a famous person and the rest of the group must guess who it is.

Mark's notes

This is a good activity to encourage pupils to see things from the perspective of their reader. It also lends itself to the notion of 'show don't tell', which could be a good way into teaching figurative devices such as simile, metaphor, imagery or onomatopoeia. (Stick that one on your spelling list!) If this is the intention, think about reading for these features earlier in the sequence, and explore how different writers and poets bring their characters to life using these devices.

For your more-able writers, encourage them to aim for subtlety and avoid clichés. (We all see them regularly: as big as an elephant, as cold as ice, as loud as thunder, and so on.) A teacher I was working with had set a brilliant task: she wanted her pupils to empathise with a homeless character, so they were taken outside, asked to build a shelter and then sat alone in the elements. They felt, listened, watched, touched. The sense of empathy in the group's writing was incredible. One pupil, though, had used a cliché: 'I felt as lonely as a cloud'. I've seen worse but felt he could do better. I asked him if there was anything he remembered from the experience which he could use for his simile. After some thinking and discussion, he came up with: 'I felt as fragile as the brittle twigs which sheltered me'. That's the power of one good thinking question.

CHARACTER BUILDING ACTIVITY

THINK about the characters in your favourite books. How does the writing help you to get to know these characters? Creating convincing characters can be more important than the story itself, and describing the little details about a character can be very powerful.

READ the extracts below and **TALK** to your partner about what you could infer about the characters from the details or hints about them:

> *She had checked the numbers on the lottery ticket she held between cracked and dirty fingertips countless times, but checked again, before blowing warm air into her cupped hands.*

He thanked the guard, brushed away the crumbs from his breakfast and smoothed out his pressed tunic. Quietly and calmly, he puffed his chest out and strode down the prison corridor to the courtyard, where the firing squad waited.

> *The pride was well fed at last and most were settled for the night. Old Primerius patrolled the perimeter, relieved to have made the kill but now feeling every painful step. He scanned the horizon and sniffed the evening air. Clinging to the familiar wafts of wild sage and distant bush fires was something unknown. What was that? He slackened his aching jaw to let the air filter through his lips, inhaling the unfamiliar smell.*

Choose a character from a piece of your own writing and ask yourself a selection of the questions below about the character:

How does their voice…

How do the things they like…

How do their belongings…

How does their hair…

How do the words they choose…

How does what they are reading…

How do their clothes…

How does their facial expression…

How does their location…

How does their movement…

How do their habits…

How do their eyes…

How do their actions…

How does their smell…

How do their fingers…

How does what they are carrying…

How does their hat…

How do their shoes…

… show the reader something about them?

Select your best ideas and **WRITE** them into your piece, including the fine details of the character for the reader to get to know them.

TOP TIP:
Show the reader, don't tell them everything.

Igniting Children's Writing © Mark McCaughan, 2018

SPEECH DETECTIVE

In this activity, pupils think about how speech and dialogue can help to develop character for the reader.

Pupils will learn:

☑ to listen well.

☑ how to think about their reader's needs.

☑ about shifts in formality.

☑ that characters and people with different ages, regional accents or characters may speak differently.

Preparation:

1 Photocopy the pupil page, enough for one each, and display it on your interactive whiteboard. This works well as a laminated mat for repeat use.

2 Model some examples of things you've heard spoken during the week.

Take it further!

- Share the outcomes of the listening task as a whole class. You could hang a washing line and create a 'continuum of formality'.

- Collect examples of things heard in school and let pupils guess who said them.

- Use the speech detective mat during a listening activity: as pupils are listening to a play scene, a monologue, a scene from a film, a radio interview. There are some great resources on **www.bbc.co.uk/learning/schoolradio** to inspire you.

Mark's notes

When I assess writing, I find that another weaker area tends to be the quality of the speech and dialogue. Often, this fails to develop its own voice, or lacks authenticity. Sometimes, pupils close to Greater Depth Standard fall short in this area. This is a shame, because good speech and dialogue can be the vehicle for evidence across the English curriculum. If, for example, a pupil writes well in role as different characters from a text, this is excellent reading evidence. As for writing evidence, good speech and dialogue is an opportunity to find assessment evidence for punctuation, vocabulary choice, shifts in formality, different sentence structures and verb forms to name but a few.

Through listening carefully, pupils may also find that speech and dialogue are where you find some of the sentence types that are less prominent in some texts: commands, exclamations and questions.

As with all areas of English teaching, it's important to write off the back of reading tasks, so focusing on how different writers use speech and dialogue, and how different characters speak, is something to do regularly.

SPEECH DETECTIVE ACTIVITY

Why do writers include speech or dialogue (speech between two or more people)? **TALK** to your partner about how and why speech is used in different types of writing. **READ** the dialogue below and **THINK** about what the reader learns about each character from how they speak:

"Yep?" barked Dad down the telephone. "Hang on a tick… ALFIE! Take your sister's head out of that bin! How many times do I have to tell you?"

"Good evening, I should like to speak with Phillip," said the voice at the other end of the line.

"No Phillip 'ere," said Dad. "Who's speaking, treacle?"

"It's the Queen. I'm awfully sorry; I seem to have the wrong number."

"Did you say Nadine? ALFIE! For crying out loud, the dog doesn't want to be painted!"

"I'm afraid one is mistaken. It's not Nadine, it's the Queen. Of England, don't you know. I am enquiring as to the whereabouts of my husband. He is required forthwith to walk the corgis."

Dad, who wasn't easily shocked, was shocked. "I am so terribly sorry. Please accept my humble apologies for the misunderstanding. ALFIE… There now, be a well-behaved young man. Goodbye, Your Majesty."

So, using speech can be very effective, but how do people *actually* speak? Let's go on a listening treasure hunt! Complete the activity below over a few days, listening to as much real speech as possible and noting down any good examples you hear.

Listen out for something very formal.

Listen out for when someone uses a funny name for something.

Listen out for something very informal.

Listen out for an interesting word or phrase which you could use in your writing.

Listen out for a word you don't know and need to look up.

Listen out for something a younger person might say.

Listen out for an idiom (a word or phrase which means something different from its literal meaning).

Listen out for something that gives a clue about where someone is from.

Listen out for something that gives a clue about how someone is feeling.

Listen out for something an older person might say.

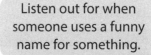

WRITE some dialogue in a play script between two characters, without stage directions. Using only the character's speech, try to give your reader a real sense of each character.

👍 TOP TIP:
Listen to how people really speak, and try to write believable dialogue.

HOW, WHERE AND WHEN ADVERBIALS

In this activity, pupils think about the effect of adverbials and how to take advantage of these in their own writing.

Pupils will learn:

☑ aspects of grammar in context.

☑ how to structure their sentences in different ways.

☑ how to think creatively about bringing their writing to life for the reader.

☑ that adverbials can be placed in different parts of a sentence for different effects.

Preparation:

1 Photocopy the pupil page, enough for one each, and display it on your interactive whiteboard. This works well as a laminated mat for repeat use.

2 Model some examples of things you've heard spoken during the week.

Take it further!

- Focus on one type of adverbial only, e.g. time, manner or place, depending on the nature of the writing task.

- Apply the same activity to a different genre. This works nicely with instructions, but could work equally well for a story, a report, a biography, a diary entry – in fact, most types of text.

- Add to the number of rows for an extended text, or reduce them for a shorter text, such as a summary.

- Establish some writing protocols, e.g. pupils draft on alternate lines, leaving every second line blank. This way, they can edit their work later in the sequence without making it too messy!

Mark's notes

This activity allows pupils to plan the main body of a text and then work around this main body. Not only will they have to practise their adverbials but pupils will have to consider the tense and form of their verbs as they construct their adverbials.

The seeds planted herea are those of the writer's craft: building up a piece of writing over time, choosing words carefully, using your reading influences, drafting ideas, changing your mind, thinking about the structure of the whole text and which of the ideas work best and where to put them.

The activities themselves will generate some great writing evidence and are bound to support the pupil to a better-quality final piece.

HOW, WHERE AND WHEN ADVERBIALS ACTIVITY

THINK about adverbials and how we can use them to give more detail about the verbs in our sentences. They are used in many ways but mainly to describe *how*, *where* and *when* verbs are being performed.

Now **TALK** to your partner about what you could add to the sentence below to add a sense of *how*, *where* or *when* for the reader.

The treasure map had disappeared.

READ the plan for a five-sentence piece of writing below:

How, where or when?	Title: How to Annoy your Brother	How, where or when?
	Sneak into your brother's bedroom.	
	Replace his signed picture of Stormzy with a Little Mix poster.	
	Put his computer games into fairy story DVD cases.	
	Hide his TV controller.	
	Deny everything.	

Now for the fun part! **READ** the version below and **TALK** to your partner about how the adverbials change the effect of the sentences.

How, where or when?	Title: How to Annoy Your Brother	How, where or when?
Waiting until he's left for football practice,	sneak into your brother's bedroom.	
After stepping over the piles of underwear on the floor,	replace his signed picture of Stormzy with a Little Mix poster.	
	Put his computer games into fairy story DVD cases	on the bookshelf beside the football programmes.
Then,	hide his TV controller,	chuckling to yourself about the misery this will cause.
When he gets home,	deny everything,	looking and sounding completely innocent.

Note that you don't have to fill in every box – it's up to you to decide what works best! Also, you will have to change the sentence punctuation when you add the adverbials.

Make three columns on your page. **WRITE** your own five-sentence piece in the middle column, then add the adverbials around it.

TOP TIP:

This works well with instructions but could also be used to draft a story, write a biography, a sports report or anything else you can think of!

E

EDIT, PERFORM, PUBLISH

EDIT WHEELS

In this activity, pupils think about the changes they can make to their draft work as they start to edit towards a polished final piece.

Pupils will learn:

☑ editing skills.

☑ aspects of grammar, e.g. parentheses, clauses, phrases, adverbials.

☑ how to ask evaluative questions about their work.

☑ to select and reject different writing choices.

Preparation:

1 Photocopy the edit wheels onto stiff card, enough for one between two. These are a great addition to the pupils' writing toolkit, so laminating them for repeated use is recommended.

2 Model a couple of examples to show pupils how you are thinking about the task and editing a draft.

3 Depending on how you choose to use the wheels, pupils may need a dice, some scissors or a counter. You can also buy board game spinners or probability spinners very cheaply, and these work well for this activity.

Take it further!

- Ask pupils to make their own edit wheel based on their personal writing targets.

Mark's notes

With the curriculum's emphasis on drafting and editing, it's important to teach these skills explicitly. The following activities are fun ways for pupils to edit their draft work.

These activities also ensure that the end piece is influenced more by the pupil and less by the teacher. This will make assessment less arduous for you because the expectation is that mistakes are being 'weeded out' of the writing through self-assessment before it gets to you. Likewise, it's more likely that your feedback can be positive and developmental rather than dwelling on those 'non-negotiables' that you may find yourself nagging about. A suggested list for display is:

- Have I checked my spelling?

- Does each sentence start with a capital letter?

- Does each sentence end with one punctuation mark?

- Is my handwriting neat and readable?

EDIT WHEELS ACTIVITY

THINK about the final stages of the writing process, when you are getting ready to publish or perform your writing. The editing wheels below can be useful as you look to improve your draft and make it as good as possible. **READ** the instructions on the wheel and **TALK** to your partner to check that you both understand what each grammatical term means.

Choose the wheel which you feel would work best for the piece of writing you are editing.

You can use the wheels in different ways:

- Use them as an ideas mat as you edit your work.

- Use as a dice game, moving a counter around the circle as you edit.

- Make a spinner or spinning top. To do this, neatly trim the edge of each sector to make a six-sided shape. Then, punch a hole in the middle and insert a short pencil, ready to spin away!

'HOT' WHEEL

- Select and improve a word.
- Select and improve a phrase.
- Select and improve a sentence.
- Find and check three words which might be spelt incorrectly.
- Change the effect of a sentence by changing its structure.
- Start a sentence or paragraph differently.

'SPICY' WHEEL

- Add some additional information within parentheses.
- Turn a single word into a phrase.
- Find any unnecessary words and take them out.
- Add a conjunction and a clause.
- Add an adverbial for manner, place or time.
- Change the effect of a sentence by change its length.

WRITE Choose a paragraph from your own writing which you feel needs some editing. On a sheet of lined paper, edit the paragraph, making the changes needed to improve it. When you're happy with the changes, stick the new version over the old version so that you can 'lift the flap' and compare the two pieces.

TOP TIP:

Good editing might include making your piece shorter by taking bits out.

Igniting Children's Writing © Mark McCaughan, 2018

EDITING DICE

In this activity, pupils make final changes to their piece, prompted by a dice consequences game.

Pupils will learn:

☑ editing skills.

☑ aspects of grammar, e.g. determiner, conjunctions, punctuation.

☑ how to evaluate and improve their work.

☑ to select and reject different writing choices.

☑ to talk and share ideas about different writing choices.

Preparation:

1 Photocopy the pupil page, enough for one between two, or display it on your interactive whiteboard.

2 Model a couple of dice throws to show pupils how you are thinking about the task and editing a draft.

3 Pupils will need two dice.

Take it further!

- Simplifying the game, if necessary, to a one-dice version.

- Ask pupils to write their own consequences based on their personal writing targets.

- Use this activity as a regular starter task to emphasise the impact of simple editing.

Mark's notes

It's important to emphasise the top tip to the pupils, so that they don't feel obliged to make unnecessary changes, which could spoil, not improve, a piece.

As well as providing a snappy editing task at the end of the sequence, this works brilliantly with older pieces of writing. I last used this as the end of KS2 teacher assessment deadline was looming, and asked a class to select any piece of writing from before Christmas. They were amazed and pleased by how much their writing had improved, and some decided to re-write a piece or two to bolster their range of evidence. It needn't take long and any editing can be completed in a different-coloured ink to highlight where changes have been made.

It always works well to generate some talk after this activity, asking pupils to share what they had written, what they changed and why they changed it.

EDITING DICE ACTIVITY

READ through your draft work and **THINK** about the changes you still need to make before you publish your work in your best handwriting. **TALK** to your partner about each other's work and the changes you both feel are needed.

Play the dice game below, acting on each dice throw by making changes to your work.

2-dice total	Editing consequence
2	Improve any word.
3	Improve a verb.
4	Improve a single word by making it into a phrase.
5	Improve a noun.
6	Improve a determiner.
7	Improve a sentence by adding a conjunction and a clause.
8	Remove any words which are not needed.
9	Improve a sentence by changing its order.
10	Improve the punctuation.
11	Improve an adjective.
12	Improve a sentence by adding a relative clause (starting with who, whose, that or which).

WRITE your piece up in your best handwriting, once you are confident it's as good as it can be.

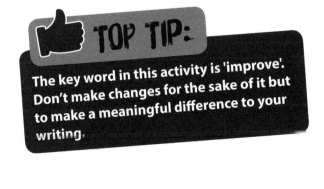

TOP TIP:
The key word in this activity is 'improve'. Don't make changes for the sake of it but to make a meaningful difference to your writing.

DETECT AND CORRECT

In this activity, pupils make a final check of their spelling as they prepare for 'publishing' their writing.

Pupils will learn:

☑ to check and edit their spelling.

☑ to spell key words.

☑ to approach words with confidence.

☑ how to construct and deconstruct words.

☑ to use a dictionary as part of their spelling routine.

Preparation:

1 Photocopy the pupil page, enough for one between two, or display it on your interactive whiteboard. This works well as a laminated mat for repeated use.

2 Model a couple of examples to show pupils how you are thinking about the task and posing questions about your spelling. It's very powerful for pupils to see that the teacher checks his or her spellings – we all do, and it's perfectly normal.

3 If you like this activity, details of how to order a complete set of Thinking Spelling resources can be found at **www.mcmlearning.co.uk**. These work best printed onto A3 and laminated for repeat use.

Take it further!

- Use this activity as a whole-class starter to revise words from yesterday/last week/last month/last year.

- Turn real words into nonsense words and then give them humorous meanings.

- Ask pupils to add words they've learnt to a personal spelling fan or onto the working wall.

Mark's notes

This activity was shamelessly pinched from my brilliant colleague Emma Dwyer. She read a library's worth of spelling theory (summary: learning spelling is multi-faceted, combining phonics, analogy, rules and patterns, sensory devices, etc.), told me about it over a a cup of tea and a chocolate biscuit, and I combined these in the Detect and correct activity.

Hopefully, I've emphasised the importance of working on words throughout the sequence. This type of activity can help us to provide a daily recycling of learning spelling, making maximum use of those transition times, start-of-day routines and extension tasks. The more high-quality exposure to words they receive, the more confident the pupils should become.

DETECT AND CORRECT ACTIVITY

How can we **THINK** about words to help us find and correct any remaining spelling mistakes? We can think about how our words look, how they sound, what they mean or which patterns we can find between words. **TALK** to your partner about the following words – what clues can you find in the words which could help us to learn them?

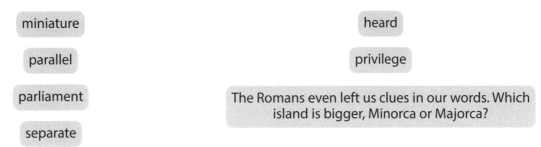

miniature

parallel

parliament

separate

heard

privilege

The Romans even left us clues in our words. Which island is bigger, Minorca or Majorca?

READ your work and highlight any words which are spelt wrong, or which need checking. Once you have checked, and found some mistakes, use the Detect and correct activity below to learn from your mistakes. (If you haven't made any, are you choosing words which are challenging enough?)

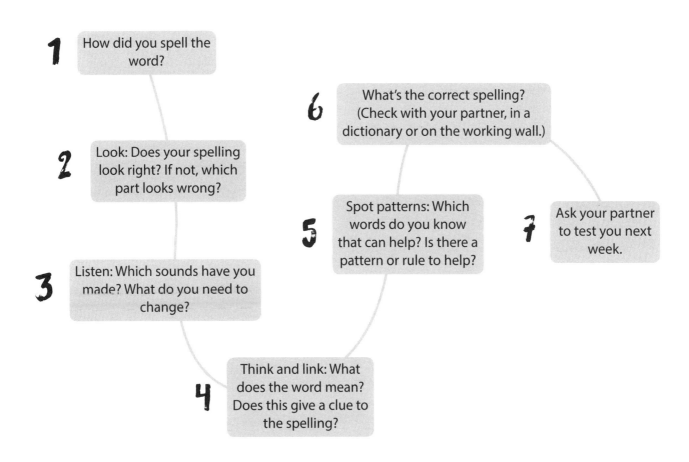

1 How did you spell the word?

2 Look: Does your spelling look right? If not, which part looks wrong?

3 Listen: Which sounds have you made? What do you need to change?

4 Think and link: What does the word mean? Does this give a clue to the spelling?

5 Spot patterns: Which words do you know that can help? Is there a pattern or rule to help?

6 What's the correct spelling? (Check with your partner, in a dictionary or on the working wall.)

7 Ask your partner to test you next week.

WRITE your spelling corrections onto your work in a different colour of pen so that they stick out as a reminder for you.

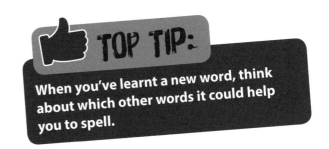

TOP TIP:

When you've learnt a new word, think about which other words it could help you to spell.

WORD EXPLOSION

In this activity, pupils 'explode' a word to learn its spelling. Over time, they will start to select the strategies which match their learning style or preference.

Pupils will learn:

- ☑ to check and edit their spelling.
- ☑ to spell key words.
- ☑ to approach words with confidence.
- ☑ how to construct and deconstruct words.
- ☑ to use a dictionary as part of their spelling routine.

Preparation:

1 Photocopy the pupil page, enough for one each. This can work well as a laminated mat for repeated use with whiteboard pens.

2 Model a couple of examples to show pupils how you are thinking about the task and using the word explosion activities.

Take it further!

- Ask pupils to make their own explosion activity based on their preferred learning style.

- Use the questions as a display or a question fan.

- Share strategies such as these with parents, so that there is consistency between home and school.

- For instant inspiration for other ways to make spelling more kinaesthetic, visit **www.pinterest.co.uk** and search 'spelling'. Other great ideas from the site include word scribbles, missing letter clip-sticks, spelling twister and gel/sand activities.

Mark's notes

This works well on the back of the other spelling activities in the sequence, especially when a pupil continues to struggle with a particular word. If this is the case, it may be that they need to experience more practical strategies, such as drawing the shape of the word, or deconstructing it into a word pyramid.

If nothing else, re-visiting spelling towards the end of the sequence reinforces the importance of accuracy in the final piece. Spelling continues to be a barrier to pupils reaching the expected standard, and it's very frustrating when it's clear that spelling routines have not sufficiently challenged or supported the pupil.

WORD EXPLOSION ACTIVITY

READ the word explosion questions below. **THINK** about the meaning of the words and **TALK** to your partner about them. Look up any words you're not sure of. What about *mnemonic*?

Now **THINK** about a word you keep getting wrong and have found difficult to learn. Look up the correct spelling of this word (a good opportunity to practise your dictionary skills) and **WRITE** it down, ready to be 'exploded'. Try out the activities around your word and see which one helps you to learn it.

What are the first and last sounds?

....

Can you think of an action to help you remember the word?

....

If you can spell this word, which other words could you spell?

....

Can you draw the word, the shapes in the word or the tricky part of the word?

....

Can you make a mnemonic out of the word, or just the tricky part?

....

Can you close your eyes and spell the word backwards?

....

What does the word mean?

....

TOP TIP:

Think about which of the activities above helped you to learn the word. We all learn differently – you may like drawing the shapes of letters and words; thinking about the sounds in words; or even making actions to help you remember. However you learn a word, the most important question to start with is always 'what does the word mean?'.

EDIT PUGS

In this activity, pupils act as critical friends to one another, peer-assessing each other's work before a final edit.

Pupils will learn:

☑ how to peer-assess and give developmental feedback.

☑ how to make meaningful changes to their work through editing.

☑ to consider the needs of their reader.

Preparation:

1 Photocopy the pupil page, enough for one each, or display it on your interactive whiteboard.

2 Model a couple of examples to show pupils how you are thinking about the task and using the Edit pug categories.

Take it further!

- Rehearse this as a whole-class task by reading a text together and then collating the feedback.

Mark's notes

Recently, I was working with a group with the potential to be a Greater Depth Standard for writing. We started the 45-minute lesson with this task, and they completed it in pairs. I had explained to them that the task was to make meaningful changes to an old piece of writing. One girl had selected a diary entry she had written six months before. There, she had written:

"Today I was walking through the woods when I suddenly saw some soldiers. I walked up to a barbed wire, I couldn't believe my eyes. I saw dozens of skelenton like children staring at me like soulless statues. Suddenly they started asking for food I said no sorry I turnt away and walked back home."

Her partner commented that her punctuation was missing at times and that it wasn't equally strong all the way through.

Following the Edit pugs activity, she wrote:

"As I was walking through the woods, I noticed some soldiers. I decided to follow them. I heard voices of children; they were laughing. Some were crying. I got closer and closer, until I spotted something horrifying."

This is shorter, more accurate, more mature, more precise, more in control, and just simply better. The activity is challenging but it works. A few weeks later the pupil was awarded Greater Depth standard at moderation.

EDIT PUGS ACTIVITY

You may think that pugs are cute and cuddly but a little-known fact is that they are ferocious editors! **THINK** about editing your draft. Swap work with your partner – you are both going to be 'edit pugs'. **READ** through each other's writing and complete the sheet below. Take your time – it's important that an editor gives clear and honest feedback. **TALK** to one another about the feedback, and take turns to explain your comments.

The pugs want to check:	🙂	☹️	Before you publish, you'll need to:
Easy to read Is the text presented well?			
Delivered the success criteria Has the writer achieved what they were aiming to achieve?			
Interesting all the way through Is the writing consistently good?			
Tone Are the tone and style of writing matched to the audience and purpose?			
Planned and well organised Is the text divided into paragraphs, sections, headings, sub-headings, etc.?			
Used a variety of sentences Is there a good mix of single and multi-clause sentences? Is there a selection of statements, commands, questions and exclamations?			
Grammar Has the writer made good grammar choices? (Tense, verbs, phrases, etc.)			
Spellings Does the writer need to work on spelling? Is there a pattern of mistakes you can help them with?			

WRITE a response to the feedback. Re-write your draft, or the parts that need some work, trying to keep the edit pugs happy! It's a good idea to edit in a different colour so that you can see your progress.

TOP TIP:

You can save time and energy by checking through your own writing before handing it to the edit pugs. A good way to do this is to read your writing aloud.

RV

REVIEW KEY
LEARNING

THE FINAL HURDLES

In this activity, pupils think about their achievements and review their key learning.

Pupils will learn:

- ☑ to read, think and talk about writers' choices.
- ☑ to assess their progress.
- ☑ to have fun with words.
- ☑ how to review their learning and consider their next steps.

Preparation:

1 Photocopy the pupil page, enough for one between two, or display it on your interactive whiteboard.

2 Model an example of each of the dice throws to show pupils how you are thinking about the task responding to the tasks.

3 Pupils will need a dice.

Take it further!

- Change the tasks – how about: odd one out, charades, hangman, a wordsearch, A–Z of key words, taboo, two truths and a lie, 20 questions.

Mark's notes

They've planned each charted course, each careful step along the byway. And more, much more than this, they did it their way. And now the end is near… Oh stop it! If they've been guided through the sequence, the pupils will have plenty to celebrate and review by this stage. So, before rushing onto the next task or unit, let the pupils secure what they've learnt and have a bit of fun along the way.

This activity generates rich talk about writers' choices and revises a bit of grammar. Then, pupils look ahead to their next steps and consider revising their targets. Finally, they put their heads together to set a challenge about the key learning in the sequence in the form of a quiz, a crossword clue or a spelling task.

This is good learning, and the third roll, especially, will be an opportunity to practise important skills such as setting out a text in different ways; using a range of punctuation; asking different types of questions; and being creative with words.

THE FINAL HURDLES ACTIVITY

It's time to review your learning, so **READ** through your finished piece. **THINK** about what writing skills you have learnt as you have built up your piece of writing.

The activity below will help you to **TALK** to your partner about your key learning. You will need a dice to help you select your three 'final hurdles'. Your first roll decides which activity you should complete from the first box. When you have completed this (take your time – it's not a race), roll the dice a second time, and so on. The third activity involves setting a challenge for another pair, so when you have finished three challenges, find another pair to exchange challenges with.

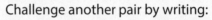

1ST ROLL

Take it in turns to show your partner:

1 the writing choice you are most proud of and why.
2 your favourite sentence and why it's your favourite.
3 your favourite phrase and why it's your favourite.
4 your favourite verb and why it's your favourite.
5 your favourite adjective and why it's your favourite.
6 your favourite paragraph and why it's your favourite.

3RD ROLL

Challenge another pair by writing:

1 a crossword clue for a key word from the writing or topic.
2 a true or false question about the writing or topic.
3 a multi-choice question about the writing or topic.
4 three tricky words for a spelling test.
5 an anagram of a key word from the writing or topic.
6 three quiz questions about the writing or topic.

2ND ROLL

Talk together about:

1 a writing skill each of you has made progress in.
2 something else each of you would like to write next.
3 something each of you would like to read as a result of your learning.
4 how each of you would summarise your pieces in 20 words or fewer.
5 a question each of you would still like to ask.
6 something each of you would do differently next time.

TOP TIP:

As well as celebrating the things you've done well, don't forget to challenge yourself with some difficult questions: Did I work hard enough? Did I plan effectively? Is the writing I have produced my best effort? What were the mistakes to avoid next time? After all, as Professor van Helsing reminds us in Bram Stoker's novel Dracula: 'We learn from failure, not from success!'

TARGET SETTER

In this activity, pupils think about their achievements and review their key learning.

Pupils will learn:

☑ to assess their progress.

☑ how to review their learning and consider their next steps.

☑ to select different success criteria for different tasks.

Preparation:

1 Photocopy the pupil page, enough for one each, and display it on your interactive whiteboard.

2 Model how to use the table – especially how to set next steps which are realistic and achievable.

Take it further!

- Introduce this into teaching sequences later in the year, when there is likely to be a greater range of evidence.

- Add a column for peer assessment; although thoughtful pairing will be required.

Mark's notes

We get to number 49 out of 50 before I must admit some mixed feelings about an activity. The reason? I think there's a fine balance to be struck between effective self-assessment (for learning) and the type of assessment which completely saps the life out of the learning. I am wary, for example, of Year 6 pupils having to paste the descriptors of the assessment framework into their books. These are aimed at teachers and only intended to support teacher assessment at the end of the key stage. If we're not careful, we become a slave to the descriptors and turn our assessment into a tick-box exercise.

This activity, however, offers a list of skills for pupils to aim for and assess themselves against. At any one time, they could have, for example, two or three targets which they aim to meet in the current piece of writing. Over time, they can show their progress as they master the skills. It's intended to be informal and developmental and not the assessment version of the Sword of Damocles looming over the pupils as they write.

TARGET SETTER ACTIVITY

THINK about yourself as a writer. **TALK** to your partner about which writing skills you can do accurately and independently, and which skills you still need to work on. **READ** through the 'I can' statements below and tick the most appropriate column for each skill.

My writing skills ('I can' statements)	In my writing, there is a range of evidence that I can do this accurately and independently	This is a target because I need more evidence that I can do this accurately and independently
Word and presentation skills		
I can use a dictionary to check words and learn meanings.		
I can use a thesaurus to make different word choices.		
I can use the classroom environment to select and learn words.		
I can use my knowledge of spelling patterns to spell age-appropriate words accurately.		
I can write quickly, fluently and legibly.		
I can select different words for a range of effects.		
I can make phrases in different ways for different effects.		
Sentence skills		
I can use different verb forms for different effects.		
I can select the appropriate verb form for different tenses.		
I can construct my sentences differently by making different grammar choices for different effects.		
I can use different types of sentence, and dialogue, to describe settings, characters and atmosphere.		
I can use the full range of punctuation marks in my year group's curriculum.		
Whole-text skills		
I can use my reading skills to select my own writing choices.		
I can plan my writing by researching, note-taking and organising my ideas.		
I can create cohesion in different ways within and between paragraphs.		
I can structure and present my writing in different ways.		
I can evaluate my own and others' writing.		
I can proof read to identify errors.		
I can edit my writing, making changes to enhance the effect and clarify the meaning.		
I can read and perform my writing aloud to different audiences.		

SUMMARY BULLSEYE

In this activity, pupils talk about their key learning and peer-assess the quality of this talk.

Pupils will learn:

☑ how to talk fluently.

☑ how to review their learning and consider their next steps.

☑ how to link different areas of learning.

Preparation:

1 Photocopy the pupil page, enough for one each, or display it on your interactive whiteboard.

2 Model an example using key learning from a previous topic to show pupils how you are thinking about the task and how a partner would assess your talk.

Take it further!

- Use this to prepare pupils for speaking and listening assessment tasks, including: delivering a speech; reciting a poem; taking part in a debate; performing a dramatic monologue. If the talk counts for assessment, you may find the standard of the talk increases. Any written preparation (scripts, notes, etc.) is also great writing evidence.

Mark's notes

This Is another activity inspired by the outstanding School 21 in Newham, London. For details of training opportunities and |many other ideas visit their website (**www.voice21.org**). I'd recommend visiting this school to see and feel the impact they've had by making oracy one of the cornerstones of their curriculum. Talk counts for something in every lesson and this type of task would feel perfectly 'normal' to the pupils there.

Pupils will find this activity difficult to start with but the initial discomfort will fade with practice. This practice is good for writing too – after all, we are actually talking when we write. The skills required (staying focused on a theme, using key words and phrases, developing a point, and linking ideas) can only improve a pupil's writing.

Pupils may also struggle in terms of giving honest and constructive feedback. Teach them to deliver a 'praise sandwich': praising a positive feature, then highlighting something to work on, and finally finishing with some more praise.

SUMMARY BULLSEYE ACTIVITY

THINK about how to summarise what you've written. **READ** through your finished piece and identify the theme of the writing; the key words and phrases; and the key ideas, facts, arguments or information. These should be the things which are crucial to summarising your text. Draw your own summary bullseye – nice and big! Then **WRITE** the words and phrases you thought of onto your bullseye.

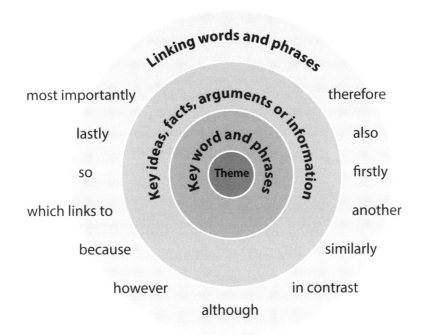

TALK with a partner; take it in turns to summarise your writing using your summary bullseye. One partner talks for up to one minute while the other partner (who will need to be able to see the summary bullseye) scores using the table below:

Award points whenever your partner:	Tally	Total
mentions the **theme** of the writing (2 points)		
uses a **key word** or **phrase** (2 points)		
mentions a **key idea/fact/argument/information** (2 points)		
uses a **linking word** or **phrase** (2 points)		
Take points away whenever your partner:	**Tally**	**Total**
says 'um…', 'err…', 'like', 'basically', 'you know', a long pause, etc.		
Overall total =		

TOP TIP:

Talking and presenting fluently is an important skill and requires lots of practice, so don't worry if you don't feel confident to start with!

Igniting Children's Writing © Mark McCaughan, 2018

ACKNOWLEDGEMENTS

Mark would like to thank the current and former English team at East Sussex County Council for their ideas, support and inspiration. They are Jane Branson, Deborah O'Donoghue, Suzy Buist, Emma Dwyer, Kathy Korpe and the brilliant Ken Haworth, who first encouraged Mark to put pen to paper.

Thanks to ROSPA for permission to use text and images from their website at **www.rospa.com** which appear in this book on p.55.

Thanks to William Sutcliffe for his permission to use an extract from *The Wall* which appears in this book on p.34.

Thanks also to Voice School 21, Newham, London, for allowing me to adapt their Summary bullseye (p. 111). For inspirational case studies about the impact of teaching oracy, visit **www.21trust.org**.